C000007656

Folens

English

The series concentrates on the basics of the English language.

The activities are straightforward, brief and to the point. They offer repetition and progression, providing a firm grounding in the language.

Each book covers: Writing
Spelling
Grammar
Comprehension

© 1997 Folens Limited, on behalf of the author.

United Kingdom: Folens Publishers, Apex Business Centre, Boscombe Road, Dunstable, LU5 4RL.
Email: folens@folens.com

Ireland: Folens Publishers, Greenhills Road, Tallaght, Dublin 24.
Email: info@folens.ie

Poland: JUKA, ul. Renesansowa 38, Warsaw 01-905.

Folens publications are protected by international copyright laws. All rights are reserved. The copyright of all materials in this publication, except where otherwise stated, remains the property of the publisher and author. No part of this publication may be reproduced, stored in a retrieval system, or transmitted, in any form or by any means, for whatever purpose, without the written permission of Folens Limited.

This resource may be used in a variety of ways. However, it is not intended that teachers or children should write directly into the book itself.

The publisher hereby asserts their moral right to be identified as the author of this work in accordance with the Copyright, Designs and Patents Act 1988.

Editor: Hayley Willer
Layout artist: James Brown

First published 1997 by Folens Limited.
Reprinted 2002.
Reprinted 2003.
Reprinted 2004.

Every effort has been made to trace the copyright holders of material used in this publication. If any copyright holder has been overlooked, we should be pleased to make any necessary arrangements.

British Library Cataloguing in Publication Data. A catalogue record for this book is available from the British Library.

ISBN 1 85276 016–8

Contents

Folens English

Teachers' notes

This series introduces pupils to the salient features of English grammar. The series develops their ability to comprehend written passages and utilises both grammar and comprehension in a series of relevant and structured exercises. The passages have been carefully chosen to give a wide variety of interesting material drawn from both fact and fiction.

How the books are constructed

Comprehension

The passages are of varying length and complexity. The pupils are asked a series of questions. In some cases the answers are explicit in the passage while in others they are implicit. Some questions go beyond the confines of the passage and draw on the pupils' more general experience and skills. In addition there are a number of exercises that are designed specifically to encourage pupils to look for meaning in writing rather than merely to decode words.

Grammar

The only grammar introduced is that which will enhance the pupils' style of writing and speech. Grammar is not treated as an end in itself; technical names for parts of speech, for example, are not used at this level. Each point is introduced by a brief explanation and followed by several sets of reinforcement and consolidation exercises.

Written style

In each book there are several sections that aim to broaden and develop the pupils' written style. These vary from drawing attention to over-used words and suggesting alternatives to extending sentence construction. In this book we concentrate on broadening the pupils' written vocabulary through a series of structured exercises.

How to use these books

Each book contains more work than you are likely to need in one school year. You will probably need to be selective, either by concentrating on one particular aspect of the book (for example grammar or style) or by deciding that it is not necessary for the pupils to complete every exercise.

The comprehension passages, in particular, lend themselves to a number of different approaches. They can certainly be used by the individual pupil and can also be used by groups, thus providing the basis for useful discussion. They could also be used as oral exercises. By starting with some of the shorter passages the teacher could provide a progressive course in listening skills.

Nature and the passage of the seasons provide the major linking themes throughout the book. The teacher may find it useful to use this material to stimulate direct observational work of the pupils' own environment. Perhaps they could keep an illustrated nature diary.

Whatever you decide to do, you will find that this series, as well as providing a core scheme, enables the teacher to achieve a high degree of flexibility of approach.

© Folens (not copiable)

Self portrait

A) Fill in the blank spaces

My name is _____ . My friends call me

_____ . I am _____ years of age.

I have _____ eyes and _____ hair.

My height is _____ and my weight is

_____ . I live in _____ with my

_____ . I have _____ brothers and

_____ sisters. I like to play _____

with my friends after _____ . My favourite

hobby is _____ . I have a fine collection of

_____ . I should like very much to be

_____ when I grow up.

B) Complete your diary

Date   Important events in your life.

For example:

1985   *Born in Bristol Regional Hospital.*

1986   _____

1987   _____

1988   _____

1989   _____

1990   _____

1991   _____

1992   _____

1993   _____

1994   _____

1995   _____

1996   _____

1997   _____

1998   _____

C) My best friend

Write a description of your best friend.

Remember to mention: age, height, likes, dislikes, colour of hair and eyes, dress, habits.

A brave dog

The dog at once jumped from the bank and in a few seconds reached the child and caught it firmly. Then he turned to swim back, but the swift-flowing water had got hold of him. Bravely he struggled and lifted the child out of the water but his powerful efforts to stem the current were in vain. Each moment he was carried still further down until he was on the brink of the fall, which, though not high, was the most dangerous on the river. He raised himself high out of the stream with the vigour of his last struggle and then fell over into the abyss.

By this time the poor mother, as if she had anticipated the result, was already in a canoe, as close to the fall as it was possible for her to go with safety. The little bark danced like a cockle-shell on the turmoil of waters as the mother stood with uplifted paddle and staring eyeballs awaiting the reappearance of the child.

The dog came up instantly but alone, for the dash over the fall had wrenched the child from his grasp. He looked around eagerly for a moment and then caught sight of a little hand raised above the boiling flood. In one moment he had hold of the child again, and, just as the prow of the mother's canoe touched the shore, he brought the child to land.

The mother sprang to the spot, snatched the child from him and gazed in anguish on its deathlike face. Then she laid her cheek on its cold breast and stood motionless. After a few moments she was conscious of some slight movement in the little body and a gentle motion of the hand. The child still lived! Opening up her blanket she drew the covering close around the child, and sitting down on the bank, wept aloud for joy.

A) Questions: Answer in sentence form where possible.
1. How do you know that the current was very strong?
2. Why did the dog not swim with the current when rescuing the child?
3. How can you tell whether the mother's canoe was above or below the fall?
4. What suggests that the dog was (a) very strong, (b) very intelligent?
5. How can you tell from the passage that the dog could act very quickly?
6. Why did the mother herself not rescue the child?
7. Why, in your opinion, did the mother place her cheek on the child's breast?
8. How did she know that the child was still alive?
9. Explain: vigour, turmoil, wrenched, eagerly, anguish, canoe, stem, anticipated.
10. Write each of the words in (9) in a sentence of your own.

   © Folens (not copiable)

Making sense

Remember: A sentence begins with a capital letter and ends with a full stop.

A) Rewrite these jumbled words to form correct sentences.

1. dress the wore a ballerina pretty beautiful.
2. bicycle won superb he racing the.
3. three fishing bought ago I a days new rod.
4. road on the slipped icy lady the old.
5. goal he football the winning the in scored game.
6. bookshop in Colette exciting novel bought the an.
7. girl won first prize the the small.
8. lap the overturned racing third on car the.
9. novel read the an man interesting.
10. cards we the morning hours until early the played of.

B) Write the following three words in an interesting sentence.

Example: sneaked, fox, clever: The clever fox sneaked into the chicken coop at night.

1. hopped, kangaroo, baby.
2. sprang, lion, majestic.
3. leaped, squirrel, shy.
4. stalked, cat, sleet.
5. barked, dog, faithful.
6. trotted, donkey, strong.
7. glided, snake, slimy.
8. galloped, horse, noble.
9. grunted, pig, fat.
10. charged, bull, magnificent.

15/08

C) Rearrange the following sentences in the correct sequence.

Everyone laughed at their funny antics.
The ringmaster was the first to appear in the centre of the ring.
They wore baggy trousers and tall red caps.
I hurriedly bought my ticket at the box office.
As I sat down, the band struck up a lively tune and the show began.
When he cracked his whip, three clowns tumbled into the ring.
A young lady showed me to my seat in the front row.

'A' and 'an'

Rules

'A' is used

a) Before consonants   e.g. a boy, a pen.
b) Before 'ew'.   e.g. a ewe, a ewer.
c) Before 'one' and 'once'.   e.g. a one letter word, a once great man.
d) Before an aspirate 'h'.   e.g. a house, a hen.
e) Before 'eu' when it is given the long 'u' sound.   e.g. a Eurasian, a European.
f) Before the letter 'u' when sounded like 'eu'.   e.g. a union, a university.

'An' is used

a) Before words that begin with a vowel.   e.g. an ugly face, an oyster.
b) Before a silent 'h'.   e.g. an honest man, an hour.

A) Choose 'a' or 'an' to fill the blank spaces in the following sentences.

1. The girl ate _an_ egg and _a_ sausage for her breakfast.
2. My brother saw _an_ owl and _a_ eagle in the forest.
3. I saw _a_ aeroplane disappear behind _a_ white cloud.
4. The carpenter had _a_ axe and _____ saw in his hand.
5. She gave the boy _____ apple and _____ orange.
6. My sister Pauline is _____ actress and my sister Jane is _____ model.
7. I have _____ uncle and _____ aunt in New York.
8. The waitress wore _____ apron and _____ white cap.
9. _____ ant and _____ flea are two tiny insects.
10. The gardener planted _____ elm tree and _____ oak tree in the garden.
11. She gave the lady _____ rose and _____ orchid.
12. _____ ewe is _____ female sheep.
13. _____ axe is _____ useful weapon.
14. _____ onion is bigger than _____ pea.
15. _____ ugly earwig crawled under _____ mossy stone.
16. I have _____ yellow canary and _____ tame rabbit.
17. John saw _____ otter and _____ beaver near the big dam.
18. Mary saw _____ unusual animal and _____ enormous elephant in the zoo.
19. _____ hour later I visited _____ ancient castle.
20. _____ apricot is smaller than _____ cucumber.
21. _____ eulogy was given at the graveside.
22. _____ ostrich and _____ albatross are two large birds.

© Folens (not copiable)

Group terms

A) Write one name for each of the following groups.

1. daffodil, rose, tulip, lily.   Flowers
2. beetle, bee, midge, locust.   _____ .
3. salmon, trout, herring, mackerel. _____ .
4. carrots, beetroot, cabbage, turnips. _____ .
5. corn, oats, barley, wheat.   _____ .
6. lark, sparrow, magpie, canary.   _____ .
7. plums, peaches, pears, pineapples. _____ .
8. palm, hawthorn, maple, lime.   _____ .
9. wine, beer, brandy, cider.   _____ .
10. panther, lynx, jaguar, cheetah.   _____ .
11. alligators, lizards, crocodiles, snakes. _____ .
12. greyhounds, huskies, pointers, alsatians. _____ .

B) Fill in the blank spaces with one of the words from the list given.
(flock, herd, gaggle, team, litter, swarm, brood, clutch, pack, nest)

1. A _____ of geese waddled across the road.
2. A _____ of chickens slept in their warm nest.
3. A _____ of dogs chased the young lambs.
4. A _____ of horses galloped across the valley.
5. A _____ of rabbits had their warren in the corner of the field.
6. A _____ of bees landed on the tree.
7. A _____ of cattle was grazing in the field.
8. The woman had a _____ of eggs in her hand.
9. The farmer admired his _____ of sheep.
10. The sow had a fine _____ of piglets.

C) Write an interesting sentence to include each of the following phrases.

1. A pack of wolves.
2. A troop of monkeys.
3. A herd of elephants.
4. A pride of lions.
5. A tribe of goats.
6. A team of horses.
7. A sloth of bears.
8. A nest of rabbits.
9. A down of hares.
10. A skulk of foxes.

© Folens (not copiable)

✓ Creative writing

A) Write an interesting paragraph about each of the following animals. Some helpful words are given.

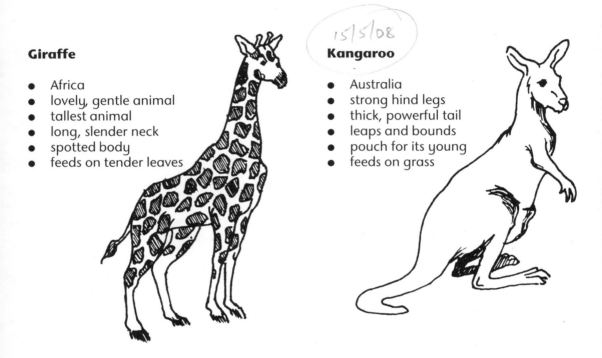

Giraffe

- Africa
- lovely, gentle animal
- tallest animal
- long, slender neck
- spotted body
- feeds on tender leaves

Kangaroo

15/5/08

- Australia
- strong hind legs
- thick, powerful tail
- leaps and bounds
- pouch for its young
- feeds on grass

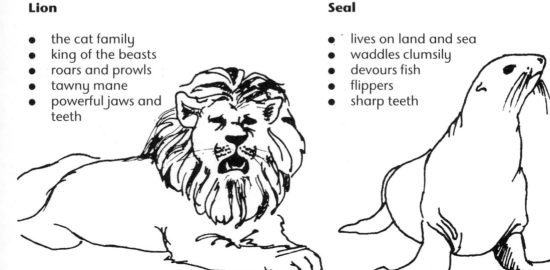

Lion

- the cat family
- king of the beasts
- roars and prowls
- tawny mane
- powerful jaws and teeth

Seal

- lives on land and sea
- waddles clumsily
- devours fish
- flippers
- sharp teeth

© Folens (not copiable)

The snake

On another day, as we were going back to the camp in the evening, Toto had wandered some ten metres in front of me, when suddenly a small snake slid out from behind a stone, passed right in front of Toto, and dropped into a crack between two rocks. Toto yelled with terror, then ran back to me, and stood, with his teeth chattering, holding his hand as if to show where he had been bitten. I examined it carefully, but could not see the tiny mark that would have been made by the snake's fangs. I made sure of this, and then told Toto that he was only frightened, and that the snake had not touched him. He did not believe me. He had been so scared by the sudden sight of the snake that he was certain that he was hurt and probably imagined that he was going to die. Knowing that this was not so, I tried to coax him to come back with me to camp. He would not come. I walked ahead, expecting him to follow. After a few paces, I looked back and saw the little fellow stretched out on the ground, convinced that he was too ill to move, and looking at me with piteous entreaty not to leave him. So I picked him up and carried him to my tent, where at last the sight of a bunch of bananas distracted his thoughts until he forgot his terror; and half an hour later he was sitting on my bed, playing as contentedly as ever.

A) Questions: Answer them in sentence-form where possible.
1. Was Toto a dog, a boy, or a monkey? Give a reason for your answer.
2. What was it that frightened Toto?
3. How did Toto show his fear?
4. 'I made sure of this'– he made sure of what, and how did he do it?
5. 'He did not believe me' – what is it that he did not believe?
6. 'After a few paces, I looked back' – what did the writer see when he looked back?
7. Why had he to carry Toto back to the tent?
8. Explain: his teeth chattered; distracted his thoughts; the snake's fangs; piteous entreaty.
9. Can you find any reason for thinking that this incident did not happen in Ireland?
10. 'Toto wandered _____ in front of me'. Write two sentences of your own, one of which will contain the word 'wandered', and another the word 'wondered'.
11. Toto was 'scared', 'terrified', 'frightened'. Which of these words suggests the least degree of fear?
12. What is the past tense of the verbs: forget, bite, sit, hold, try, come, drop.

Capital letters

Capital letters begin the names of **weekdays**, **months**, **festival days**, **places** and **people**.

A) Insert the capital letters where needed.
1. Next sunday is easter sunday.
2. Uncle james gave me a present last tuesday.
3. My brother went to rome last wednesday to see the pope.
4. I saw the president of france while in paris.
5. Last june I visited my aunt shona.
6. He travelled to spain on new year's eve.
7. Mr murphy is the lord mayor of our town.
8. Uncle richard's birthday is in may.
9. The sixth month of the year is _____ .
10. _____ is the last month of the year.
11. _____ is the shortest month of the year.

Capital letters begin:
i) The names of places – Spain.
ii) Words derived from the names of places – Spanish.
iii) A person's nationality – Spaniard.

B) Complete the following sentences using capital letters.
1. Perhaps he is an _____ as his father lives in Italy.
2. She is a Parisienne. She comes from _____ and speaks _____ .
3. I am an Athenian. I am from _____ .
4. My friend is from Spain. He is a _____ .
5. Maybe he is from _____ as he speaks Portuguese.
6. _____ cheese is manufactured in Denmark.
7. They are Venetians. They come from _____ .
8. The Pope travelled to France and met the _____ president.
9. I am a _____ . My home is in Sweden. I speak _____ .
10. The _____ live in Finland and speak _____ .

C) Insert the capital letters where needed.
1. i am going to the cinema with george.
2. lille is an industrial city in northern france.
3. mrs flood went to london and bought a dress in harrods.
4. the bbc light orchestra provided the music at the national concert hall.
5. the president of america lives in the white house.
6. the first of april is called 'april fools' day.
7. mary is my cousin and she lives in scotland.
8. every tuesday in june she visits her aunt maureen.
9. the english team should win on saturday.

    © Folens (not copiable)

Interesting sentences

A) Complete the following sentences.

1. Yesterday _____ because it was raining.
2. Last night _____ until it was midnight.
3. Today _____ since it is very fine.
4. Last week _____ as it was a holiday.
5. Tomorrow night _____ if I have any money.
6. A fortnight ago _____ at the seaside.
7. Last month _____ and I enjoyed myself.
8. Tomorrow morning _____ because I am going away.
9. A week ago _____ when you were away.
10. Yesterday afternoon _____ as I was feeling ill.

B) Write the three words in an interesting sentence of your own.
1. soldier, fought, bravely.
2. judge, listened, patiently.
3. sailor, slept, soundly.
4. pilot, decided, immediately.
5. mountaineer, fell, heavily.
6. air hostess, waited, anxiously.
7. swimmer, shouted, frantically.
8. thief, crept, silently.
9. typist, worked, diligently.
10. athlete, ran, quickly.

C) Places

(aviary, gallery, distillery, hold, nursery, zoo, surgery or operating theatre)

1. A ship's cargo is kept in a _____ .
2. Operations are performed in a _____ .
3. Young shrubs are grown in a _____ .
4. Whisky is made in a _____ .
5. Paintings are kept in a _____ .
6. Wild animals are kept in a _____ .
7. Birds are kept in an _____ .

© Folens (not copiable)

Over-used words

Do at later stage!!

A) Then

This word is used far too frequently to commence sentences. The following story is monotonous, because the word 'then' is over-used. Rewrite the story, omitting the word.

then then then Then then then then then then Then

Here is a list of useful words and phrases to help you.
(finally, eventually, next, later on, after that, subsequently, shortly afterwards, presently, at last, almost immediately, soon afterwards)

Mary carefully wrote the address on the envelope and placed the stamp on the right hand corner. Then she ran to the pillarbox at the corner of the street and dropped the letter into the box. Then her letter was on its way to her Aunt Julia. Then the postman arrived in the mail van and emptied the pillarbox. Then the mail was brought to the Post Office where it was postmarked and sorted. Then that evening all the air mail letters were placed in special sacks, and labelled 'Air Mail'. Then these sacks were carried to the main airport and placed aboard an aeroplane to New York. Then at Kennedy Airport a mail van was waiting as parcels were again sorted and placed in canvas bags for the different post offices in New York. Then the following morning Mary's letter was delivered to her aunt's apartment. Then it had reached its destination.

B) Ate

Choose a suitable verb from the list in brackets, and complete the sentence.
(licked, devoured, gulped, gobbled, sucked, chewed, nibbled, munched, pecked, gnawed)

1. The cat _____ .
2. The rabbit _____ .
3. The cow _____ .
4. The lion ___ - _____ .
5. The mouse _____ .
6. The hen _____ .
7. The turkey _____ .
8. The girl _____ .
9. The boy _____ .
10. The hungry man _____ .

  © Folens (not copiable)

Writing words

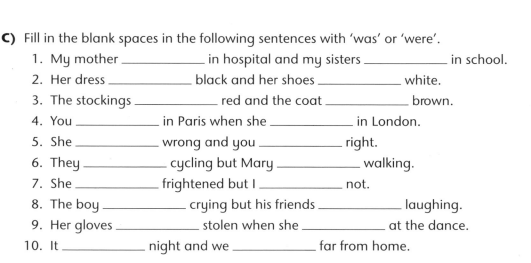

A) Find the missing letters from the clues given.
1. _ ee _ Plural of foot.
2. _ ee _ A common drink in a bar.
3. _ ee _ A period of seven days.
4. _ ee _ The opposite of the word 'shallow'.
5. _ ee _ The farmer sows it in spring.
6. _ ee _ A forest animal with antlers.
7. _ ee _ Sugar is made from this vegetable.
8. _ ee _ The skin of an orange.
9. _ ee _ A plant that grows in marshy places.

B) Find the missing letters from the clues given.
1. _ ea _ 365 days.
2. _ ea _ A group of players.
3. _ ea _ A person not able to hear.
4. _ ea _ Part of the body above the neck.
5 _ ea _ A soft heavy metal.
6. _ ea _ Foliage.
7. _ ea _ Every butcher sells it.
8. _ ea _ To cure.
9. _ ea _ Warmth.
10. _ ea _ A name for one of the glass balls on a necklace.

C) Fill in the blank spaces in the following sentences with 'was' or 'were'.
1. My mother _____ in hospital and my sisters _____ in school.
2. Her dress _____ black and her shoes _____ white.
3. The stockings _____ red and the coat _____ brown.
4. You _____ in Paris when she _____ in London.
5. She _____ wrong and you _____ right.
6. They _____ cycling but Mary _____ walking.
7. She _____ frightened but I _____ not.
8. The boy _____ crying but his friends _____ laughing.
9. Her gloves _____ stolen when she _____ at the dance.
10. It _____ night and we _____ far from home.

© Folens (not copiable)

The animal world

Animal homes

A) Complete the following sentences. (Use your dictionary to check the spellings.)

1. A dog lives in a _____ and likes to eat _____ .
2. A horse lives in a _____ and likes to eat _____ .
3. A hen lives in a _____ and likes to eat _____ .
4. A wild rabbit lives in a _____ and likes to eat _____ .
5. A sheep lives in a _____ and likes to eat _____ .
6. A hare lives in a _____ and likes to eat _____ .
7. A cow lives in a _____ and likes to eat _____ .
8. A pig lives in a _____ and likes to eat _____ .
9. A fox lives in a _____ and likes to eat _____ .
10. A mouse lives in a _____ and likes to eat _____ .

Animal sounds

B) Choose the correct word to describe the sounds the animals make, and complete the sentence.

1. The donkey _____ when _____ .
2. The bull _____ because _____ .
3. The dog _____ until _____ .
4. The cat _____ beside _____ .
5. The lamb _____ whenever _____ .
6. The pit _____ when _____ .
7. The horse _____ while _____ .
8. The cow _____ when _____ .

Animal clothing

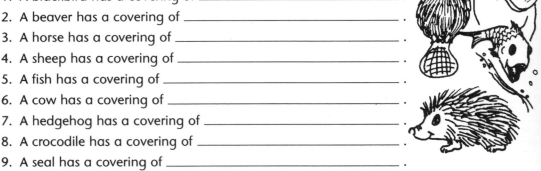

C) Name the protective covering worn by the following creatures.

1. A blackbird has a covering of _____ .
2. A beaver has a covering of _____ .
3. A horse has a covering of _____ .
4. A sheep has a covering of _____ .
5. A fish has a covering of _____ .
6. A cow has a covering of _____ .
7. A hedgehog has a covering of _____ .
8. A crocodile has a covering of _____ .
9. A seal has a covering of _____ .
10. A turtle has a covering of _____ .

© Folens (not copiable)

The wonder of words

A) –IST words

Find the missing words from the clues given. They all end in –ist.

		I	S	T				A girl who uses a typewriter.
		I	S	T				He sketches pictures.
			I	S	T			She extracts teeth.
			I	S	T			He rides a bicycle.
			I	S	T			He goes on holidays to other countries.
			I	S	T			He works in a pharmacy.
			I	S	T			She sells flowers.
				I	S	T		He drives a car.
				I	S	T		He studies plants.
					I	S	T	She writes for the newspapers.

B) 'SEE-SAW' words

Fill in the missing words from the clues given.

1. An animal that gives us mutton.
2. An oyster's covering.
3. Opposite of heavy.
4. A person with no religion.
5. Opposite of day.
6. A jungle animal.
7. A cattle farm in the U.S.A.
8. A male singer.
9. It flows into the sea.
10. Homes for bees.

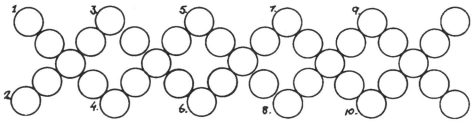

C) –ABLE words

A	B	L	E			A piece of furniture.
	A	B	L	E		A horse's home.
		A	B	L	E	Ability to do something.
			A	B	L	E	Easily carried.
			A	B	L	E	English policeman.
				A	B	L	E	Kind and friendly towards guest.
				A	B	L	E	Cannot be separated.

© Folens (not copiable)

The secret cave

A) Compose a short story beginning like this:

I had no sooner entered the mouth of the cave than a great stone door closed behind me. I was trapped inside the dark and gloomy cavern ...

Helpful words and phrases

Explored ...... ray of light ...... a stone staircase ...... amazed ...... wondrous sight ...... gleaming brass lantern ...... a wisp of curling smoke ...... the genie ...... treasure chest ...... dazzling emeralds ...... glittering jewels ...... sapphires ...... pearls ...... pitchers of golden coins ......

© Folens (not copiable)

Guru Nanak and the Banker

Guru Nanak was the founder of the Sikh religion. He was born in what is now Pakistan, in the region known as the Punjab, which means 'Land of the Five Rivers'. During his lifetime he travelled a great deal, teaching as he went.

Long ago, in the city of Lahore there lived a banker called Duni Chand. Throughout the city he was well known for his greed and dishonesty. He lived in a beautiful palace, which shone with gold, marble and precious jewels.

One day, Duni Chand heard that Guru Nanak had arrived in Lahore. He rushed out to invite him to a special feast. Guru Nanak accepted the invitation and preparations for the feast began. All the guests agreed that it was a magnificent feast. Duni Chand turned to Guru Nanak when everyone had finished, and said, "I am a wealthy man, if I can do anything for you, please tell me."

Guru Nanak sat and thought for a moment. He looked around at the splendour of the palace, the rich tapestries hanging on the wall and the fine golden dishes. He then fumbled in his pocket and took out a slim case which contained a tiny, fine needle. Holding up the needle, he replied, "Yes, there is something I would like you to do for me. I would like you to keep this needle very safely and give it back when we meet in the next world." And with these words the Guru left the feast.

Duni Chand felt full of importance. The Guru had entrusted him with such a special task. He then took the needle and showed it to his wife, explaining what the Guru had told him. To his utter astonishment, she burst into peals of laughter. She laughed, "Oh, my poor husband. I should go back to Guru Nanak and ask him how you can take it to heaven with you."

Duni Chand felt rather confused, and hurried after the Guru. "Guru Nanak, Guru Nanak", he called. "Before you go, just tell me one thing. How can I take this needle with me when I die?" The Guru looked at Duni Chand kindly and said, "If you cannot take a tiny needle with you when you die, how are you going to take all your riches? You will only be remembered for the good things you have done in this world when you go to the next." Duni Chand thought and realized the truth in the Guru's words. He felt so ashamed that from that day on he and his wife used their wealth to help the poor.

A) Dictionary work: Find out the meaning of banker, peals, splendour, tapestries, confused. Write each one in a sentence of your own.

B) Questions
1. Why was the banker well known?
2. Why did Duni Chand hold a feast?
3. What did Guru Nanak give to Duni Chand?
4. Why did Duni Chand feel important?
5. What did Duni Chand's wife think of Guru Nanak's gift?
6. What does Guru Nanak say we will be remembered by?
7. Use your atlas to find out where Lahore is.
8. Rewrite the story setting it in modern times.

Nouns

A noun is a naming word. It names some person, place, animal, state or thing;
e.g. A pack of dogs frightened the sheep in the field. Tom and Mary ate pancakes
with their friends. The colour of the ink is black.

A) In the following passage pick out twenty-seven nouns.

It was a glorious September day, with the warm sun shining brightly in the blue sky.
High up in the air, the lark was filling the heavens with melody, and from tree and
hedge came the sweet notes of thrush, blackbird and robin. The sheep were lying
peacefully in the shade of the trees, and the cows were knee-deep in the river.
Down in the valley, the machines were noisily cutting the golden corn; but louder
than the noise of the machines were the shouts of the children bathing in the cool
pool by the ash grove.

B) Underline the nouns and
pronouns in the following sentences.

1. Preston is a town in Lancashire.
2. John Bond won a silver medal in Los Angeles.
3. John Treacy won a silver medal in Los Angeles.
4. The chain was made of gold.
5. The dog likes to eat meat and chew bones.
6. Last Friday we ate fish for dinner.
7. A spade is made of metal.
8. Tom uses a tractor when ploughing, but John uses a team of horses.
9. He managed to escape under cover of darkness.
10. Stirling is a beautiful town in Scotland.
11. A plague of locusts ate all the wheat.
12. The girl chopped wood for the fire.
13. The Czar of Russia had great wealth.
14. Rabbits eat grass, but otters eat fish.
15. We breathe air into our lungs.
16. The fisherman filled his basket with fish.
17. A pack of hungry dogs attacked the sheep.
18. The owner of the hotel is a wealthy lady.
19. Joan kept her pet parrot in a cage.
20. The ship struck a reef, but the crew was saved.
21. The King lives in peace and safety with his family.
22. It is a treasure of great beauty.

© Folens (not copiable)

Exercises

A) A 'pygmy' is a very small person.
Write an interesting sentence about the following types of people.

1. miser _____
2. coward _____
3. hero _____
4. rogue _____
5. tyrant _____
6. hermit _____
7. giant _____
8. tycoon _____
9. hypocrite _____
10. optimist _____
11. pessimist _____
12. egoist _____
13. glutton _____

GIANT HERO
EGOIST
HYPOCRITE
MISER
COWARD
ROGUE
hermit
PESSIMIST

CONSULT YOUR DICTIONARY

B) Choose a suitable word from the given list to complete the phrase. Write each phrase in a sentence. (tribe, river, shoe, clock, chair, bottle, saw, needle, hill, corn)

1. the leg of a _____ .
2. the brow of a _____ .
3. the tongue of a _____ .
4. the mouth of a _____ .
5. the neck of a _____ .
6. the teeth of a _____ .
7. the eye of a _____ .
8. the face of a _____ .
9. the head of a _____ .
10. the ear of _____ .

C) Write suitable words at the start of each of the following sentences.

1. _____ because he was not well.
2. _____ but I am much better now.
3. _____ when I fell on the glass.
4. _____ so she went to the dentist.
5. _____ when he touched the hot plate.
6. _____ if he had enough money.
7. _____ since the last game.

© Folens (not copiable)

Silent letters

A) Examine the following list of words and underline the silent letter in each.

1. climb
2. scene
3. sign
4. height
5. heir
6. knit
7. should
8. calf
9. solemn
10. psalm
11. empty
12. aisle
13. apostle
14. wren
15. doubt
16. abscess
17. knob
18. talk

B) From the clues given find the right word; then underline the silent letter in the word.

1. A young sheep. l_____
2. A man who repairs pipes. p_____
3. A grave or monument. t_____
4. Used to arrange your hair. c_____
5. An odour or smell. s_____
6. Land surrounded by water. i_____
7. A sailing boat. y_____
8. A small bird. w_____
9. The yellow of an egg. y_____
10. A sacred song. h_____
11. The opposite of 'son'. d_____
12. The third season of the year. a_____
13. A wild animal with horns. r_____
14. A young cow. c_____
15. Sixty minutes. h_____
16. To hurry. h_____
17. A king's symbol of power. s_____
18. To divide in two equal parts. h_____
19. Sharp-bladed weapon. s_____
20. A morsel of bread. c_____
21. A garland of flowers. w_____
22. Slender stem of a plant. s_____
23. A red berry fruit. r_____
24. A tiny, winged insect. g_____
25. The opposite of 'native'. f_____
26. A prickly plant. t_____
27. Joint in the leg. k_____
28. Charity and help. a_____

© Folens (not copiable)

Word meanings

A) Some words have the same spelling and pronunciation but different meanings. Give at least two meaning for each word below. Use a dictionary to help you if necessary.

Example:

bark: Sound made by a dog.
Outer covering of tree.

ball: _____

calf: _____

crab: _____

flock: _____

habit: _____

bay: _____

page: _____

crop: _____

deal: _____

fair: _____

left: _____

race: _____

pupil: _____

pen: _____

moor: _____

pole: _____

pale: _____

pike: _____

pitch: _____

sole: _____

rest: _____

ring: _____

sack: _____

yard: _____

shed: _____

season: _____

lime: _____

box: _____

butt: _____

bait: _____

meal: _____

post: _____

firm: _____

Creative writing

A) Late for school
Write a suitable ending to the following story.

It was the ticking of my alarm clock that finally wakened me. I glanced in horror at the time. It was nine o'clock.

Helpful words and phrases
rushed down the stairs ...... gulped my food ...... pedalled furiously ...... dodged in and out ...... rounded a corner ...... swerved to avoid ...... hoot of a horn ...... screech of brakes ...... arrived breathless ......

Finish the following stories (there are useful words and expressions on page 94 which can be of help).

B) Forbidden fruit

I crept slowly along the wet branch. My trembling hands grasped the slippery bough. The sweet juicy apples were within my grasp ...

C) The hungry wolf

It was a cold and bitter winter. Snow covered the mountain tops. Food was scarce. The lean and hungry wolf howled at night. At last, he was forced to leave his den and search for food in the valley below ...

© Folens (not copiable)

A lesson learned

As Paul rushed out of the school gate, he was thinking of the football game and the fact that he was the team captain. He raced home in order to get changed. Just then a big lorry went slowly past the school gate. It was travelling in his direction. He could not resist the temptation of a short ride. He ran and jumped on the back of the lorry. "How lucky I am," he thought, as he clung to the back.

On reaching the top of the hill, the vehicle picked up speed. Houses and trees seemed to flash by him. He did not dare not let go. He hung on desperately for one kilometre, two kilometres. At last, the vehicle slowed down as it chugged its way up a hill. Paul took his chance and dropped to the ground. He landed with a thud and fell awkwardly. He felt a sharp pain shoot up his right leg. He stood and tried to run, but collapsed on the ground and groaned in agony. A passer-by phoned for an ambulance, and within minutes it arrived and took him to the nearest hospital. His leg was put in a plaster, and he spent many weeks in hospital. The doctor told him he had fractured a bone in his ankle but luckily for him he would be able to play football again. Paul was sorry that he had let his team-mates down, and given his parents a terrible shock. Too late, he had learned a lesson he would never forget.

A) Questions: Answer them in sentence-form where possible.
1. Why was Paul hurrying home from school?
2. How far did he go on the lorry?
3. Why did he not jump off?
4. What happened to Paul's leg?
5. Who phoned for the ambulance?
6. What valuable lesson for life did Paul learn?
7. What did his school companions think when he failed to turn up for the game?
8. Draw a poster for a Road Safety Competition.
9. What are the colours of traffic lights?
10. Write four rules of the road that are important to pupils going to school.

    a. _____

    b. _____

    c. _____

    d. _____

© Folens (not copiable)

Masculine and feminine

A) Write the masculine form of the words in italics.
1. *Mother* and *aunt* were laughing.
2. The *princess* spoke to the *queen*.
3. The *lady* wore *her* new hat.
4. The *wife* went to see *her hairdresser*.
5. My *sister* waved to *Louise*.
6. The *heroine* thanked the *stewardess* for *her* help.
7. The *countess* greeted the *duchess*.
8. The *woman* handed *her daughter* a cheque.
9. The *girl* spoke to the *nun*.
10. The *waitress* served *Mrs Carroll*.

B) Write the feminine form of the words in italics.
1. The *prince* greeted the *actor*.
2. The *headmaster* has a *son* in my class.
3. His *nephew* is a famous *man*.
4. My *grandfather* was a great athlete when *he* was young.
5. The *landlord* is a *bachelor*.
6. The *waiter* gave *him* a fright.
7. The *man* thanked *his host*.
8. The *bridegroom* waved to *his brother*.
9. The *manager* gave instructions to the *steward*.
10. The *shepherd* gave Joseph a present of a *ram*.

C) Fill in the blank spaces in the following chart.

	Masculine	Feminine	Young
1.	deer	_____	_____
2.	lion	_____	_____
3.	_____	tigress	_____
4.	_____	vixen	_____
5.	_____	_____	cub
6.	bull seal	_____	
7.	stallion	_____	_____
8.	_____	leopardess	_____
9.	_____	she-bear	_____

© Folens (not copiable)

Birds

A) Take note of the verbs used. Finish the sentences.

1. The owl hoots at night in _____ .
2. The lark sings in _____ .
3. The wren warbles so as to _____ .
4. The eagle screams when _____ .
5. The pigeon coos while _____ .
6. The robin chirps if _____ .
7. The swallow twitters on _____ .
8. The blackbird whistles when _____ .
9. The parrot screeches whenever _____ .
10. The crow caws early _____ .

B) Choose an appropriate adjective from the given list to describe each of the birds and finish the sentence.
(proud, tireless, tiny, gentle, little, graceful, swift, tawny)

1. The _____ robin hopped from _____ .
2. The _____ owl flitted across _____ .
3. The _____ lark soared high in _____ .
4. The _____ blackbird flew into _____ .
5. The _____ eagle swooped down _____ .
6. The _____ swan flapped her wings when _____ .
7. The _____ seagull glided towards _____ .
8. The _____ wren hopped along_____ .

C) Write the opposite of the words in italics.

1. The bird flew to the *North Pole*.
2. The sea was very *calm*.
3. The boy trapped the *wild* pigeon.
4. She is a *lazy* bird.
5. The *young* swallow was found *dead* in her nest.
6. The *wild* birds *arrived* during the *night*.
7. He *refused* to *open* the door of the cage.
8. He *captured* the *fat* penguin.
9. The swallows *disappeared* at sunset.
10. Every *evening* the eagle watches the sun *sinking* in the *west*.

© Folens (not copiable)

Confusing words

'Learn' or 'teach'

> To learn – means to acquire knowledge or skill by study, practice or teaching.
> To teach – means to instruct or give knowledge.

A) Fill in the blank spaces in the following sentences with either 'teach' or 'learn'.

1. Let her _____ you how to swim.
2. If you _____ the lessons, you will pass the examination.
3. We _____ the same lessons as the girls.
4. If I _____ to cycle, I will _____ you during the Christmas holidays.
5. Try to _____ quickly. Then you will be able to _____ your brother as he is very slow to _____ .
6. The captain likes to _____ the junior boys how to _____ to ride properly.
7. He likes to _____ the girls how to _____ to dance gracefully.
8. She will _____ to play the guitar if you _____ her slowly.

'To', 'two', 'too'

> 'To': shows movement towards; e.g. He is going to school.
> 'To' also indicates the infinitive of a verb; e.g. She hopes to win a prize.
> 'Two': Is a number; e.g. The two boys are with two girls.
> 'Too': Means 'also', 'enough', 'more than enough', 'likewise' etc; e.g. The inspector asked too many difficult questions.

B) Write either 'to', 'two', or 'too' in the correct places.

1. David is _____ ill _____ go _____ the pop concert.
2. The last _____ days were _____ wet _____ play games.
3. The teacher told me _____ leave for home at _____ o'clock.
4. John went _____ the dance and Mary went with _____ of her friends.
5. My _____ sisters travel _____ school by bus.
6. I am going _____ the film today with my _____ cousins.
7. I am _____ young _____ be admitted _____ the dance.
8. It is _____ early _____ retire _____ bed.
9. The question was _____ hard _____ answer.
10. It is _____ soon after dinner _____ go swimming.
11. The teacher ordered _____ of us _____ play in the game.
12. If you are going _____ the pop concert may I come _____ .
13. The _____ of us were _____ tired _____ play in the garden.
14. The teacher showed the pupils _____ ways _____ solve the problem.

© Folens (not copiable)

At the circus

A) Write an essay on a visit to a famous circus.

Helpful words and phrases

the gaily-uniformed band ...... the ringmaster's arrival ...... performing ponies ......
ridden by pretty girls ...... trotted ...... bowed ...... pranced ...... swish of their tails ......
the brave lion-tamer ...... breathtaking act ...... deathly silence ...... head in lion's
mouth ...... loud applause ...... the comical clowns ...... funny antics ...... turning
cartwheels ...... feast of fun and laughter ...... daring trapeze artists ...... somersaulted
...... flirted with death ...... dancing elephants ...... thundered around the arena ......
aquatic skill of the seals ...... balancing objects ...... tight-rope walker ...... bicycle and
balancing pole ...... the strong man ...... feats of strength ...... thrilling moment when
...... high divers ...... the fire-eaters ...... the magician ...... the performing dogs ...... the
football game ......

In this essay avoid the use of the word 'then'. The following words and phrases can be
used to begin sentences.
(first, soon afterwards, next, almost immediately, shortly afterwards, presently, no
sooner had, than, later on, at the interval, in the meantime, finally)

The Marie Celeste

As Captain Morehouse climbed up onto the deck of the Dei Gratia, on the morning of the 8th of December, 1872, little did he realise that one of the greatest mystery stories of all time was about to unfold before his eyes. Thankfully the Atlantic crossing had been smooth and uneventful, and the Dei Gratia was now less than three hundred kilometres from her destination, Gibraltar. The quiet thoughts of the captain were suddenly interrupted by eager cries of "Ship ahoy! Ship ahoy!" – one of the crew had spotted a ship coming towards them on the starboard side. Quickly snatching his telescope, Morehouse soon observed that there was something strange about this ship, for she was steering wildly and lurching through the waves. And what was even more disconcerting, nobody appeared to be on deck! The alarmed captain immediately sent four of his men out by rowing boat to board the ship and investigate. A search of the ship confirmed that there was nobody aboard. The ship was the Marie Celeste which had set sail from New York a month earlier.

No clue could be found as to the crew's disappearance. There was plenty of food and water aboard; all the crew's belongings were neatly packed in their sea chests; and furthermore, there was no sign of any violence having taken place. When Captain Morehouse sailed into Gibraltar with the Marie Celeste, it caused a sensation, and a full enquiry was ordered without delay. Did the crew mutiny? Were they attacked by pirates? Was some mysterious illness responsible for their disappearance? Or could a giant sea monster have swept them all overboard?

These and many other questions were asked, but no conclusive answer was ever found to explain the mystery of the Marie Celeste.

A) Questions: Answer in sentence-form where possible.
1. Where was Captain Morehouse on the morning of the 8th December, 1872?
2. What was the destination of the Dei Gratia and how many more kilometres did she have to travel?
3. How were the Captain's thoughts interrupted?
4. What alarmed Captain Morehouse about the ship he saw?
5. Describe what action he took in order to investigate the ship.
6. What was the name of the ship, and from where did she come?
7. Pretend you are one of the sailors sent to investigate the ship. Describe what you saw when you went on board.
8. What happened when the captain sailed into Gibraltar with the Marie Celeste?
9. Write your own ideas or theory as to what must have happened to the crew of the Marie Celeste.
10. Find out the meaning of these words: starboard, lurching, disconcerting, conclusive.
11. Write each of the above words in a sentence of your own.

© Folens (not copiable)

Singular and plural

Singular means one.
Plural means more than one.

A) Give the singular of the following words.

1. armies _____	5. feet _____	9. mice _____
2. foxes _____	6. tomatoes _____	10 oxen _____
3. fairies _____	7. roofs _____	11. geese _____
4. thrushes _____	8. loaves _____	12. teeth _____

B) Rewrite these sentences in the plural.
1. The man captured the robber.
2. The woman sang a song.
3. The fisherman caught a trout and a salmon.
4. The shepherd watched over his flock.
5. The knife is on the shelf.
6. The lady gave a present to the child.
7. The farmer felled the tree in the field.
8. The mouse escaped from the trap.
9. The potato was too big to cook with the tomato.
10. The thief stole the watch.
11. The wolf killed the sheep.
12. The fox attacked the goose.
13. The man ate the trout.
14. The woman screamed when the mouse appeared.

C) Rewrite the following sentences in the singular.
1. The women picked the tomatoes.
2. The flies landed on the bushes.
3. The men were afraid of the women.
4. The thieves stole the watches.
5. The donkeys had sore hooves.
6. The dwarfs lived in the valleys.
7. The children picked the leaves.
8. The dishes were on the shelves.
9. The mice lived in the pianos.
10. The potatoes were the same size as the oranges.
    (If you are in doubt about any of the answers to the above exercise, read the 'rules' on page 32).

Plural of nouns

A) Here are some general rules for the formation of the plural of nouns. Read them and then write the plurals of the following nouns.

Rule		Example	

1. Most nouns simple add –s to the singular. **pen** ☞ **pens**   ruler _____

2. Nouns ending in –s, –x, –sh, –ch, or –ss form their plural by adding –es to the singular.

box _____   church _____
glass _____   brush _____

3. Nouns ending in –f or –fe in general change the –f or –fe into –v and add –es.

loaf ☞ **loaves**   hoof _____
knife ☞ **knives**   life _____

Common exceptions: chief, safe, gulf, cuff, proof, reef.

cliff ☞ **cliffs**   **roof** ☞ **roofs**

4. Nouns ending in –y preceded by a consonant change the –y to –I and add –es. Otherwise add –s.

lady ☞ **ladies**
baby _____
fly _____

5. A small number remain unchanged in the singular and plural.

sheep *stays as* **sheep**
deer *stays as* **deer**
Other examples: **salmon, cod, snipe, plaice, mackerel, trout**

6. Some nouns ending in –o add –es for the plural, others add –s. There is no simple rule – learn each new word.

potato ☞ **potatoes**
hero ☞ **heroes**
pianos ☞ **heroes**

7. Some nouns have no singular.

scissors, shears, suds, measles, pliers, pants, tongs, trousers, thanks, bellows, tweezers, spectacles, pincers

B) Write the following sentences in the plural.
1. The boy worked in the city. _____
2. The goose was killed by the fox. _____
3. The hero saved the lady. _____
4. The thief stole the ruby. _____
5. The mouse ate the cheese. _____
6. The army dug the trench. _____
7. The man chased the donkey. _____
8. The wolf devoured the sheep. _____
9. The calf hid behind the bus. _____
10. The tomato in the box is rotten. _____

© Folens (not copiable)

Exercises

The orange grove

A) Read the following story carefully, and then write six questions about it.

Yesterday, Pedro and Isabella had great fun in the beautiful orange grove. The day was sunny and warm and suitable for the orange-picking. How lovely the golden fruit looked, hanging from the green orange trees!

Isabella enjoyed picking the fruit. She wore gloves to save the skin of the oranges from being spoilt, otherwise they would arrive at the greengrocer's shop all soft and unfit to eat. Her brother, Pedro, climbed the ladder and picked the oranges from the top of the tree. "Just imagine, Isabella," said Pedro, "this orange I'm picking may be eaten by an English boy." At noon, their father arrived with the truck to collect the baskets of fruit they had picked. He was very pleased with their work. They quickly loaded the fruit on to the truck. Their father allowed them to travel with him to the market in Madrid. How happy they were, as they sped along the dusty road towards the big city.

B) Containers for food

Underline the correct word in brackets. Write each phrase in a sentence.

1. A (*jug, can, bowl*) of sugar.
2. A (*cup, kettle, pan*) of coffee.
3. A (*box, goblet, bottle*) of milk.
4. A (*basin, chest, barrel*) of tea.
5. A (*sack, pot, chest*) of jam.
6. A (*keg, bowl, bucket*) of beer.
7. A (*can, vase, sack*) of flour.

C) Underline the correct word in brackets.

1. He bought a (*bunch, pot, cup*) of grapes in the fruit shop.
2. The girl carried a (*barrel, basket, bowl*) of fruit in her hand.
3. The (*herd, flock, swarm*) of bees landed on the apple tree.
4. The hungry rat ate a hole in the (*vase, sack, bucket*).
5. The lorry lost a (*crate, chest, can*) of oranges.
6. A (*shoal, pack, flock*) of hungry birds ate the cherries in the orchard.
7. The thief stole a (*box, carton, bottle*) of apples from outside the shop.
8. The (*jug, bottle, jar*) of honey fell off the counter and broke in pieces.

© Folens (not copiable)

The right word in the right place

'Got', 'get', 'getting'

> 'Got', 'get' and 'getting' are used too often in conversation and essay-writing. A more varied vocabulary is needed.

A) Rewrite the following sentences, replacing the words in bold type with one of the words in the given list.

(suggested, solving, improving, pass, lift, discard, awoke, prepared, bought, boarded, enjoy, reaches, mounted, cycling, became, arranging, plunged, developed, decreasing, increasing)

1. I got up early and got my breakfast.
2. John got on his bicycle, and succeeded in getting through the crowd.
3. They got the right ticket, but got on the wrong bus.
4. She will get a magnificent view when she gets to the top of the mountain.
5. Get the top off the box, and get rid of the contents.
6. Our emigration figures are getting smaller, but our population is getting bigger.
7. Peter is getting on well in his new school, and he hopes to get through his examination.
8. My sister got impatient while she was getting ready the flower display.
9. Anne has got the best way I know of getting over the problem.
10. After he got into the icy waters, he got a cramp in his right leg.

'Put'

> Avoid using this word in your essay-writing. Choose more exciting and interesting words.

B) Rewrite the following sentences replacing the word in italics with one from the list.

(increased, suggested, exiled, suppressed, annoyed, saved, diverted, extinguished, tolerate, postponed, cancelled, evicted, applied)

1. She *put off* her visit to the dentist.
2. He was *put off* when the referee ordered him off the field.
3. The team manager cannot *put up* with such bad behaviour.
4. The government *put up* the price of petrol.
5. The army *put down* the prisoners' revolt.
6. When the play started, she *put out* her cigarette.
7. The miser *put by* a large sum of money.
8. The traffic was *put on* another route, because of a major accident.
9. The revolutionary leader was *put out* of the country.
10. The footballer *put in* for a transfer to another club.

© Folens (not copiable)

An underwater adventure

A) Write an essay on an underwater adventure.

Helpful words and phrases

ventured into deep water ...... dangerous reefs ...... shark-infested water ...... thrilling moment ...... explored the green waters ...... moving cautiously ...... strands of seaweed ...... strange sea creatures ...... corals ...... anchor embedded in sand ...... prow ...... hull ...... battered wheelhouse ...... investigated ......

© Folens (not copiable)

Migration mysteries

The migration of birds was a source of complete mystery to people in bygone times. For example, because people never saw the nests, eggs, or chick of the barnacle goose, they could not understand how these fully-grown birds magically appeared in Britain each autumn. The best explanation given – and this was believed by all – was that barnacle geese simply hatched out of barnacles at the bottom of the sea, and hence the name.

Today, other mysteries of migration are being unravelled. At the end of each summer an estimated 4,000 million birds migrate from Europe to spend the winter in Africa and Asia. Of these, at least half will be dead by the following spring. Nevertheless, there can be no doubt but that extremely accurate navigation is involved in these journeys. Even the young cuckoo, abandoned by its parents, will still be able to travel on its own all the way back to Africa for winter. The question that puzzled scientists for so long was: how can these birds navigate so well, both by day and by night? It now seems certain that migrating birds use the position of the sun and stars, as well as their own sense of smell and sound, in finding their way. Even more fascinating is the new discovery that birds also use magnetism to navigate. Bird tissue has been found to contain magnetite, which is the basic mineral in magnets. This magnetite somehow acts on the earth's magnetic field to give the bird a sense of North-South direction. Proof of this can be seen by trapping a tiny magnet to the wings of a homing pigeon. The magnet will interfere with the bird's own magnetic sense, thus making it very difficult to find its way home. Using these varied methods in navigation, it is possible for the migrating bird to cover enormous distances with pin-point accuracy.

A) Questions: Answer in sentence-form where possible.
1. Why was the migration of birds a source of mystery to people in bygone times?
2. How did the barnacle goose get its name?
3. At what time of year do 4,000 million birds migrate from Europe, and where do they go?
4. How do migrating birds navigate?
5. What question puzzled scientists for so long?
6. What new discovery has been made about migration?
7. How does magnetite help birds to find their way? Can this be proven?
8. Name four migrant birds found in the United Kingdom.
9. Write a paragraph about birds and why you like them.
10. Find out the meaning of these words: navigate, unravelled, estimated, accurate, interfere.
11. Write each of the above words in a sentence of your own.

　　　　　　　　　　　　　　　　　　　　© Folens (not copiable)

How to address an envelope

This is how the name and address should be written on an envelope:

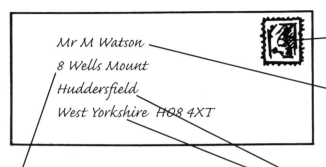

Mr M Watson
8 Wells Mount
Huddersfield
West Yorkshire HO8 4XT

1. The stamp is placed at the top right-hand corner.

2. The name should be written on the first line. Place Mr before the name when writing to a man, and Mrs, Miss or Ms when writing to a woman.

3. The street or road should be written on the second line. Many of these names can be abbreviated (shortened) if you wish. For example, 'Street' is written 'St' and 'Road' is 'Rd'. Can you write what these abbreviations mean?

Dr   _____

Ave _____

Sq   _____

Tce _____

Gdns _____

Cl   _____

4. The town is written on the third line.

5. The county is written on the fourth line.

6. If the letter is to be sent abroad, place the name of the country on the fifth line.

Note:
1. Write the name and address in good clear writing.
2. The first line of the address should start well away from the top of the envelope and a little to the right.

A) Write the address of a friend or relation on an envelope like this.

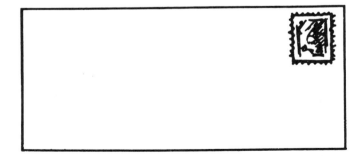

B) Draw envelopes and address them to these people.
1. Dr B Broderick, 48 Richmond Gdns, Poole, Dorset WY2 1LT
2. Miss Jean Roberts, 38 Market Square, Chester CH4 8DE
3. Mrs K Murphy, The Elms, Firgrove Lawn, Penrith, Cumbria CA11 1YT
4. Mr Peter M Kennedy, 16 Church St, Cromer, Norfolk NH3 4DE
5. Rev P Dodd, The Rectory, Greenfield Avenue, Glasgow G12 7PF

scurried **FLUTTERED** **Verbs** *crawled* **swam**

landed *wriggled*

DARTED *leaped frisked*

A verb is a word that shows action.

A) Underline the verb and finish the following sentences.
1. The bee landed on _____ .
2. The butterfly fluttered near _____ .
3. The frog swam towards _____ .
4. The trout darted across _____ .
5. The squirrel leaped through _____ .
6. The ant crawled along _____ .
7. The worm wriggled under _____ .
8. The rabbit scurried into _____ .
9. The lambs frisked and frolicked in _____ .
10. The spider ran into _____ .

B) Underline the correct verb in brackets and, write it in an interesting sentence.
1. The patient (*ran, jumped, hobbled*) around the hospital ward.
2. The postman (*swam, crept, plodded*) wearily through the snow.
3. The fireman saw the fire and (*strolled, walked, dashed*) down the street.
4. The baker (*jumped, ran, trotted*) over the low fence.
5. The soldier (*flew, galloped, marched*) across the barrack square.
6. The baby (*sprinted, toddled, strode*) across the floor.
7. The drunken man (*staggered, hurried, sprinted*) along the road.
8. The thief (*jumped, dived, prowled*) around the house.

C) Choose an appropriate verb to fill in the blank spaces in the following sentences.
1. The cornered fox _____ fiercely.
2. The old engine _____ noisily up the hill.
3. The hungry calf _____ all night long.
4. The rabbit _____ with terror as the trap _____ on his forelegs.
5. The horses _____ through the swollen river.
6. The huge wave _____ against the rocks.
7. The windows _____ loudly in the violent storm.
8. The cows _____ slowly through the marshy ground.
9. The cat _____ from her basket by the fire, when she _____ the mouse.
10. The alarm bell _____ the sailors from their sleeping cabins.
11. Slowly he _____ his way through the dense undergrowth.
12. The car _____ in order to avoid knocking down the pedestrian.

© Folens (not copiable)

Over-used words

'Walked' or 'went'

A) These verbs are too frequently used in writing. In the following sentences choose a suitable verb from the given list to replace the verbs 'walked' or 'went'. Complete each sentence.

(charged, crept, prowled, strolled, toddled, shuffled, limped, plodded, staggered, hobbled, dashed, marched, waded, stepped, sauntered)

1. The daring fireman (went) _____ quickly _____ .
2. The lame man (walked) _____ slowly _____ .
3. The young boy (went) _____ noisily _____ .
4. The brave hunter (walked) _____ stealthily _____ .
5. The injured player (went) _____ painfully _____ .
6. The weary boxer (walked) _____ helplessly _____ .
7. The old postman (went) _____ wearily _____ .
8. The clever burglar (walked) _____ silently _____ .
9. The courageous soldier (went) _____ bravely _____ .
10. The old lady (walked) _____ feebly _____ .
11. The wise fisherman (went) _____ cautiously _____ .
12. The American tourist (walked) _____ casually _____ .
13. The chubby baby (walked) _____ haltingly _____ .
14. The happy teenagers (walked) _____ slowly _____ .
15. The nervous woman (walked) _____ hurriedly _____ .

Use of 'lot'

B) This word is used to describe almost anything. Use alternative words and expressions in your writing. Rewrite the following sentences omitting the words in italics.

Choose one of the words from the given list.

(much, all, crowd, selection, many, plenty, spectators, variety, troupe, abundance)

1. After the game a *lot of people* invaded the football field.
2. The fisherman had *an awful lot of* fresh herring for sale.
3. *A lot* of people dislike spiders.
4. I bought a *whole lot of* the records.
5. The robber stole *a lot of* money.
6. There is an *awful lot* of wheat grown in Canada.
7. *Lots of* reasons were given for his poor performance.
8. The audience was entertained by a *lot of* Spanish dancers.
9. *A lot of* people in the street watched the fire.
10. *A lot of* boys in my class are going to the game.

© Folens (not copiable)

Playing with words

A) Find the phrase equal in meaning to each single word on the right.

in this place	instantly
as a rule	gradually
at the same time	seldom
at once	here
now and then	presently
in every possible place	generally
little by little	recently
in that place	occasionally
not very often	never
in a moment or two	there
not long ago	simultaneously
at no time	everywhere

B) These three words do not change if spelt backwards: eye, eve, noon.
Now find twelve others.

1. _____ 2. _____ 3. _____ 4. _____

5. _____ 6. _____ 7. _____ 8. _____

9. _____ 10. _____ 11. _____ 12. _____

C) Change the word 'ball' into 'goal' by easy stages, changing only one letter at a time. The clues will help you.

BALL

_ _ _ _ high.
_ _ _ _ a monkey uses it to swing.
_ _ _ _ to work very hard.
_ _ _ _ a roll of wire.
_ _ _ _ black rock dug out of the earth.

GOAL

D) Complete these pairs by choosing the correct word from the list given. Write your answer in the blank spaces.
(means, there, easy, go, out, ends, all, far, about, square, again, forth, parcel, thin, sound)

1. Odds and _____
2. Near and _____
3. Out and _____
4. One and _____
5. Down and _____

6. Ways and _____
7. Back and _____
8. Here and _____
9. Fair and _____
10. Time and _____

11. Free and _____
12. Touch and _____
13. Thick and _____
14. Safe and _____
15. Part and _____

© Folens (not copiable)

A beautiful view

A) Write a suitable ending to this story.

On a beautiful June day, I mounted my bicycle and headed out the country. My destination was a lovely valley nestling among the hills.

At last, hot and panting, I arrived at my destination. I dismounted slowly ...

Helpful words and phrases

the tall pines ...... a rocky hill ...... humming of birds ...... murmuring stream ...... chirping of birds ...... sparkling lake ...... winding river ...... sighing of the wind ...... rustling of the leaves ...... majestic waterfall ......

B) Write a suitable ending to the following story.

Paul saw the large-looking creature bury itself in the sand and slowly crawl under the rock. Cautiously he groped about in the sand with his fingers. Suddenly ...

Helpful words and phrases

sharp claws ...... clung to his fingers ...... pinched ...... screamed with pain ...... shook the crab ...... trickle of blood ...... crab crawled slowly away ......

C) Write a suitable ending to the story.

It was a beautiful May morning. Farmer Daly went out early to the field to count the young lambs. Just as he was about to enter the field, he spied a huge eagle soaring in the sky. Suddenly ...

© Folens (not copiable)

The Inuit

The Inuit live in the far north of Canada and Greenland. The land is covered with snow and ice nearly all the year round. They are small people with broad pale faces, slanting eyes and straight black hair.

They dislike cutting their hair as they believe it is unlucky. They wear furry hooded anoraks that have no buttons but slip on over the head. Waterproof trousers and mitts keep their legs and hands warm and dry. They often wear two pairs of long sealskin boots to keep out the cold. These swarthy people look fatter than they really are because of their thick garments.

When they go on long hunting trips in winter they build beehive-shaped huts called igloos. The igloo is made from thick blocks of frozen snow placed on top of one another. The skilful Inuit may take less than an hour to build an igloo. When not out hunting they live in modern wooden homes. Most villages have electricity, a school, a shop and an airfield!

The people are clever hunters and fishermen. They travel over the snow and ice on sledges drawn by a team of fierce dogs called huskies. Inuit also have motorised sledges called skidoos for everyday use. The Inuit hunts with a rifle although years ago they used spears known as harpoons. The seal is very valuable to the Inuit. They make tents, ropes and cord from its skin. The warm seal's blood can be drunk and seal-oil is made from the thick layer of fat or blubber that is inside the seal's skin.

In summer the Inuit goes hunting for walrus in a frail kayak. The kayak is a light wooden canoe covered with sealskin. It skims swiftly through the water. Strapped in a kayak the Inuit can turn right over in the water and come up again without sinking.

Inuit should be admired and respected for their great courage and skill.

A) Questions: Answer them in sentences where possible.
1. Where do Inuit live?
2. What colour is their skin?
3. How do they dress in winter?
4. Where do they obtain their food?
5. How do they hunt seals?
6. What means of transport have the Inuit?
7. Give another word for: 'trousers' and for 'mitts'.
8. Write an interesting sentence about each of the following:
   i) igloo, ii) anorak, iii) husky, iv) harpoon, v) kayak.
9. The walrus is an arctic creature. Name six others.

   i) _____   iv) _____

   ii) _____   v) _____

   iii) _____   vi) _____

10. Write the following words in sentences to show their meaning:
    slanting, waterproof, swarthy, garments, blubber, frail, skims.

     © Folens (not copiable)

Adjectives

Adjectives are words which describe things. An adjective is said to qualify the noun it describes. Sentences without adjectives tend to be boring – for example: 'The man was sitting in the cottage'. By adding adjectives we can get a clearer, more interesting picture of the two nouns in this sentence, the 'man' and 'the cottage'. For example: 'The little, wrinkled, old man was sitting in the small, thatched cottage'.

A) Rewrite these dull sentences by adding at least one adjective to each noun.
1. The girl was wearing a dress.
2. The bull was in the field.
3. The boy was sitting in the classroom.
4. The detective questioned the man.
5. He stopped the car in a lane.
6. They landed the spaceship on the planet.
7. I saw a clown in his costume.
8. She wrote a letter and left it on the table.
9. The horse was in the forest.
10. The liner crossed the ocean.

B) Write as many adjectives as you can for each of the following nouns. The first one is done for you.
1. mountain: rocky, snowy, dangerous.
2. dog: _____ .
3. stream: _____ .
4. lorry: _____ .
5. apple: _____ .
6. doctor: _____ .
7. lady: _____ .
8. castle: _____ .
9. book: _____ .
10. boat: _____ .

C) Choose the correct adjectives from the following list to fill the blank spaces in the story. (ancient, wild, noble, wrinkled, bright, tough, large, younger, beautiful, golden, tiny, bitter, warm, cold, cosy, soft)

She was a _____ old woman who belonged to the Cherokees, an _____ and _____ tribe of Native Americans. Her tepee was made from the _____ skins of _____ animals she herself had hunted in her _____ days. She had painted the outside with _____ designs and _____ pictures of the _____ rabbit, the _____ buffalo and the _____ eagle, and she had lined the inside with _____ furs of beaver and bear. During the _____ , _____ nights of winter she was kept _____ and _____ in her well-constructed home.

Houses

My house

A) Fill in the blank spaces with suitable words.

My house is situated _____ . It is a _____ building. Although it is
old, it is _____ . There are _____ in it. The bathroom is
_____ and painted _____ . The sitting-room is very spacious and it
has _____ windows. We do our cooking in _____ .

In the front of the house there is a lovely _____ with two flower
_____ . My mother and I take care _____ in the garden. We grow
many roses and _____ Mother has won several _____ at the Derby
Flower Show. The big garden at _____ is cared for by _____ . He
grows _____ and _____ . He enjoys _____ there. I love
my _____ very much. It is _____ to me than all the world. There is
no place like _____ .

Homes

B) State where the following people live and complete
each sentence.

1. A king lives in a _____ near _____ .
2. A monk lives in a _____ surrounded by _____ .
3. A shepherd lives in a _____ high up _____ .
4. A gypsy lives in a _____ beside _____ .
5. A soldier lives in a _____ beyond _____ .
6. A convict lives in a _____ during _____ .
7. A nun lives in a _____ near _____ .
8. A lumberjack lives in a _____ in the _____ .
9. An Inuit lives in an _____ in the _____ .

C) House for sale

FOR SALE:
Cromer. Taylor's Hill semi-
detached house in beautiful
condition, with oil-fired central
heating, garage attached,
gardens front and rear.
Jones and Smith, Auctioneers.
Tel. Cromer 36915.

Compile interesting newspaper advertisements for
the following items which you are prepared to rent
or sell:
i) Camping-tent for hire.
ii) A summer chalet to let.
iii) A bicycle to sell.
iv) A guitar or a transistor to sell.

44

© Folens (not copiable)

Confusing words

'I' or 'me'

A) Rewrite the following sentences and fill in the blank spaces with either 'I' or 'me'.

1. He pushed _____ and _____ fell into the pool.
2. She gave _____ a pear and _____ ate it.
3. The teacher asked _____ to read the book and _____ did so willingly.
4. She and _____ played the guitar.
5. The bull chased _____ and _____ jumped over the ditch.
6. The teacher told _____ to go home and _____ was delighted.
7. Mary divided the sweets between Thomas and _____ .
8. Margaret is older than _____ but _____ am taller than she.
9. The ball dropped between Peter and _____ but _____ got it.
10. She gave _____ an orange and _____ bought her an apple.

'Is' or 'are'

B) Write the following sentences and fill in the blank spaces with either 'Is' or 'are'.

1. Her hands _____ clean but her face _____ dirty.
2. My gloves _____ upstairs and my coat _____ in the hall.
3. His cheeks _____ swollen and his nose _____ cut.
4. The boy's feet _____ cold but his hands _____ warm.
5. Her eye _____ sore and her tooth _____ loose.
6. Joan's face _____ pale and her ears _____ red.
7. Her fingers _____ swollen and her thumb _____ broken.
8. When she _____ singing what _____ you doing?
9. The stranger's eyes _____ brown and her hair _____ jet black.
10. John _____ crying because his teeth _____ broken.

'There' or 'their'

i) **There** means 'in that place'. The men went **there**.
ii) **There** is used with the verb 'to be'. **There** is (was) a book on the table.
iii) **Their** means 'belonging to them', and is always followed by some noun. I lost **their** books.

C) Fill in the blank spaces with either 'there' or 'their'.

1. The swallows built _____ nests _____ last year.
2. _____ feathers are scattered here and _____ .
3. I stood _____ watching the birds building _____ nests.
4. _____ was no trace of _____ canary.
5. _____ is an owl in _____ barn.
6. The birds perched _____ with _____ friends the crows.
7. _____ are no eggs _____ yet.
8. _____ and then the hunter shot _____ tame pigeon.
9. Over _____ is a wild animal.
10. Despite _____ efforts _____ pet parrot escaped.

How to write a letter

Read the following letter carefully.

The greeting. Note the use of capital letters and the placing of a comma at the end of the greeting.
Examples: Dear Mum, Dear Mum and Dad, Dear Mary, Dear Ms Smith, Dear Sir, Dear Madam.

The writer's full address must be shown at the top right-hand side of the page. The residence, street and postal town must be included in the address. Names of houses begin with capital letters but no quotation marks ('......') are required.
Examples: Avondale, Beach Grove, Pine Wood, Meadow Court.

> Crossways
> 6 Hazel Rd
> Putney
> London SW8 5PY
> 13/6/1997
>
> Dear Harry,
>   I am enjoying my stay here with my cousins in London. Since I arrived, the weather has been sunny, and my cousins have been showing me around some of the interesting places in the city. Yesterday, we visited the National Museum, and earlier today we went to the zoo. If it stays fine, we will probably go swimming at Wimbledon Baths tomorrow.
>   I do hope that your injured leg has improved, and that you will be able to come up for the big match at Wembley on Saturday.
>
>   Your good friend,
>   *Tony*

The ending. Again note the use of the capital letter and the placing of the comma.
Examples: Your loving daughter,
Your fond son,
Your good friend,
Yours sincerely,
Yours truly,
Yours respectfully.

The message or content of the letter.

The signature.

The date must be clearly indicated. You may write the date in a variety of ways.
Examples: 3/2/1995 3/2/95 3/2/'95

A) Write out correctly the following letter.

24 High St, Tadcaster, North Yorkshire, LS24 SPF, 4th November 1997
Dear Miss Murphy, I am sorry Helen is absent from school this week. She has the measles and is still under the doctor's care. She will return as soon as she is better. Yours sincerely, Kay Ryan.

46

© Folens (not copiable)

Nanuk the bear

You may meet the Polar Bear at any time and almost anywhere – usually when you least expect him. He may be sitting at your door, or trundle across your trail when you are hunting. You may meet him along the coast, where you have gone to visit your trap lines, or even a hundred miles out in the ocean – Mr Polar Bear, calmly riding on a floating iceberg or swimming in the freezing water without effort.

The first time you see him you are shocked. An enormous fat weasel! Such is your impression of his short legs, long body, endless neck and slender snout. He weighs as much as 1,000kgs and consequently does not look active, but seems to thunder along slow and unhurried, as clumsy as can be. Do not be deceived; he is just as agile in attack as in flight, and in battle is a dangerous enemy. He can gallop when he has to, but his best gait is a trotting stride, wobbly but steady, which he can maintain all day long, provided he has not had too much to eat. Food is his weakness.

For the pleasure of gorging himself, Nanuk the Bear will take any kind of risk. He will walk right into a camp full of dogs and men, and even into a shack. In really lean days, he will steal seal right off a sled, though ordinarily he is not a thief. He is an experienced seal-hunter himself. Seal is the only food he really likes, and what he wants is the blubber. He cares little for meat, except when he is on his last legs. He loves to play, and if he finds a seal oil drum he is delighted, rolling it downhill, pushing it like a wagon, trundling it like a barrow and finally smashing it to bits, as a child will break a toy he tires of.

In winter, Nanuk will confidently go after a seal under two metres of ice. His technique is flawless. He finds the seal's breathing holes in the ice – five or six of them. He selects one and carefully digs into the ice around it. Then he covers the thin ice with snow. Then he sits down, motionless as a marble statue, his left paw poised ready to strike. He will stay at his post, as still as a rock, until the seal comes up to breathe. The bear is so intent on his task that it is quite easy to surprise and kill him while he waits. Sometimes the sly Inuit waits until he gets the seal first. As soon as the seal comes to the hole, Nanuk's paw comes down. He never misses.

A) Questions: Answer them in sentences where possible.
1. To what part of the world does the writer refer?
2. How does the writer show the strength and endurance of the bear?
3. Why might a person not used to polar bears be deceived into thinking the animal slow and inactive?
4. What might make the bear unable to trot all day long?
5. In what way does the bear resemble a child?
6. How is it shown that Nanuk is a patient and clever animal?
7. 'Sometimes, the sly Inuit waits until the bear gets the seal first.' What advantage does the Inuit gain by waiting?
8. Give the meaning of: iceberg, lumber along, filch, flawless, confidently.
9. Write each of the above words in a sentence of your own.
10. For homework, can you write ten sentences about 'Iceland'.

More adjectives

A) From the words on the left, form adjectives to fill the blank spaces.

beauty   1. The gentleman wore a _____ shirt.

courage   2. The _____ policeman rescued the little child!

expense   3. He bought an _____ suit of clothes.

power   4. He was a _____ swimmer.

fame   5. President Kennedy was a _____ man.

friend   6. The _____ dog wagged his tail.

grace   7. The _____ swan glided through the water.

victory   8. The _____ team was given a great welcome by the enthusiastic crowd.

mystery   9. A _____ man appeared at her window.

depth   10. The teenager was drowned in the _____ pool.

Use of 'good' and 'well'

Good: It is an adjective, e.g. John is a **good** soccer player.
Well: It is an adverb, e.g. John plays **well**.

B) Fill in the blank spaces in the following sentences with either 'good' or 'well'.

1. The girl is a _____ actress and she acts _____ .

2. A _____ band plays _____ when it has an audience.

3. He does not balance _____ because he is not a _____ tight-rope walker.

4. A _____ knife-thrower always throws the knife _____ .

5. The lion-tamer was in _____ humour because his lions performed _____ .

6. The _____ horse trotted _____ around the arena.

7. He is a _____ acrobat but he does not perform as _____ as his partner.

8. A _____ performance is always _____ appreciated by the audience.

Use of 'nice'.

People too frequently use 'nice' to describe almost anything.
They say: a nice girl, a nice day, a nice kitchen, a nice car.

enjoyable
interesting
attractive
delicious
fine
beautiful
pretty
handsome
comfortable
lovely

C) Choose words from the given list instead of the word 'nice'.

1. She wore a _____ dress and a _____ hat.

2. We had a _____ meal in a _____ hotel.

3. He read his _____ book in his _____ armchair.

4. The holiday was _____ and the weather was _____ .

5. The _____ lady stood near the _____ man.

                                                    © Folens (not copiable)

Usage of words

A) Write down the word that comes between each of the pairs.

1. morning _____ night.
2. summer _____ winter.
3. boy _____ man.
4. beginning _____ end.
5. sun _____ stars.
6. all _____ none.
7. breakfast _____ supper.
8. millimetres _____ decimetres.

B) Letter-changing

Change the first letter of each word to form a new word. Then change the last letter of the new word to compose another new word.

		New word	Second new word
Example	1. book	cook	cool
	2. list	_ ist	_ is _
	3. kill	_ ill	_ il _
	4. coat	_ oat	_ oa _
	5. hell	_ ell	_ el _
	6. pair	_ air	_ al _
	7. race	_ ace	_ ac _
	8. pear	_ ear	_ ea _
	9. boot	_ oot	_ oo _
	10. cell	_ ell	_ el _

C) Give one word for each of the following. Choose your answers from the list below.

1. A floating mass of ice. _____
2. A place where there is nothing but sand. _____
3. A person fleeing from the law. _____
4. A person who carries luggage in a hotel. _____
5. A person who sings alone. _____
6. A person who collects stamps. _____
7. A man who never marries. _____
8. A book that gives the meaning of words. _____
9. A person who plans roads. _____
10. A watering place in the desert. _____
11. A document which allows tourists to go from one country to another. _____

(desert, passport, philatelist, oasis, bachelor, fugitive, iceberg, engineer, porter, dictionary, soloist)

© Folens (not copiable)

Exercises

'Has' or 'have'

A) Fill in the blank spaces with either 'has' or 'have'. Write the sentences.

1. I _____ a cat which _____ a sore paw.
2. The hen _____ a nest in the hay and so _____ the goose.
3. Goats _____ horns but chicken _____ not.
4. A turkey _____ two legs but a horse _____ four.
5. My cat _____ a white tail and her kittens _____ black tails.
6. The gander _____ a long neck but the cat _____ a short neck.
7. I _____ only one stomach but the cow _____ four.
8. We have a Manx cat and she _____ no tail.
9. You _____ a dog but Mary _____ a cat.
10. The two of us _____ to work on the farm as our father _____ gone to the market.

'Of' or 'off'

B) Fill in the blank space in the following with either 'of' or 'off'.

1. The clown ran _____ with one _____ the balloons.
2. Which _____ you switched _____ the light?
3. He galloped _____ ahead _____ the rest _____ the field.
4. The rest _____ the girls saw Mary dive _____ the rock.
5. The teacher asked the two _____ us to turn _____ the water.
6. He took _____ his coat because _____ the heat.
7. I set _____ on the journey with the rest _____ the hikers.
8. The aeroplane took _____ at the end _____ the runway.
9. Several _____ the players were ordered _____ the field.
10. The younger _____ the two girls was afraid _____ the monkeys.
11. A bag full _____ flour fell _____ the lorry.

'Do' or 'does'

C) Choose 'do' or 'does' to fill the blank spaces in the following sentences.

1. What _____ you _____ on Christmas Day?
2. I _____ not know how to make the plum pudding but my mother _____ .
3. What _____ Santa Claus have to _____ on Christmas Eve?
4. Why _____ he not _____ the painting with you?
5. She _____ not know how to _____ the cooking.
6. Jane _____ her best and she cannot _____ more.
7. She _____ need plenty of rest and so _____ you.
8. _____ clean your room as it _____ looks very dirty and untidy.
9. I shall _____ the dusting and you will _____ the cleaning.
10. It _____ not matter now whether he _____ it or not.

© Folens (not copiable)

The flood disaster

A) Write an essay on the flood.

Helpful words and phrases

1. torrential rain for days ...... strong gales ...... river rising ...... isolated farm in the hills ...... danger to farmer and family ...... ducks splashing happily ...... roads flooded ...... gas and electricity failures ...... panic-stricken animals ...... farmer worked feverishly ...... the stables ...... chicken coop ...... the byre ......

2. river burst its banks ...... swirling, muddy waters ...... farmyard flooded ...... lapping water washed ...... drinking water scarce ...... farmer marooned ...... animals struggling desperately ...... family scrambled to safety ...... countryside one big lake ...... family waiting anxiously ...... hoped and prayed ......

3. clung to the roof ...... drenched to the skin ...... at last ...... noise of a helicopter ...... hovered overhead ...... relief ...... waved ...... the rescue operation ...... taken to nearest town ...... several days before floods receded ...... damage and devastation ...... a trail of destruction ...... felled trees ...... dead animals ...... flooded homes ...... floating debris ......

Gold fever

The discovery of gold in California in the last century caused an outbreak of a strange, new 'disease' known as gold fever. People became so gripped by the lure of gold that they actually showed all the symptoms of a fever – sleeplessness, restlessness and hot, nervous excitement. A side effect of this fever was a doubling of the population of California in a short space of time! One of those bitten by the gold bug was a certain E.H. Hargreaves, who travelled all of 6,500 kilometres from Australia in search of Californian gold. Unfortunately, he arrived too late. His journey was not a complete waste of effort, however, for Hargreaves spent the time in California studying the type of rock and landscape most likely to yield gold!

Equipped with this knowledge, he returned to Australia in 1851, and immediately announced to his friends that he was about to take a canoe down the Macquarie River in search of gold. His friends just laughed and said he was mad. Nevertheless, the undaunted Hargreaves set off on his expedition, accompanied by a bushman named Lister. A long, difficult journey finally brought them to a small creek along the river, whereupon Hargreaves suddenly had a strange overpowering feeling that there was gold everywhere around them. When he told Lister, the bushman was convinced that Hargreaves had indeed gone stark, raving mad. Then Hargreaves stooped down and dug up a handful of mud – it was full of glittering, sparkling gold!

When the discovery was announced in the papers on the 15th May 1851, it caused an immediate outbreak of gold fever. Thousands upon thousands deserted their jobs and rushed to begin diggings all over the countryside. Many were successful. One man dug up 15 kilograms of gold in a single hour; another found a single nugget worth £12,000, a huge sum in those days. It was Hargreaves' turn to laugh now – all the way to the bank.

A) Questions: Answer in sentences where possible.
1. What effect did gold have on people?
2. What effect did the discovery of gold have on California?
3. How did Hargreaves put his journey to California to good use?
4. Why did his friends think he was mad?
5. Did Hargreaves go alone on this expedition?
6. Give reasons why you think the journey down the Macquarie River was difficult?
7. Write six words to describe how Hargreaves must have felt when he noticed gold in the mud of the river.
8. Imagine you were in Australia when the discovery of gold was first announced. Write a paragraph to describe what you saw.
9. Use your atlas to locate the position of California in the United States and the Macquarie River in Australia.
10. Find out the meaning of these words: lure, yield, undaunted, symptoms.

© Folens (not copiable)

Adverbs

Adverbs are words which tell us more about verbs. Most adverbs are made by adding –ly to adjectives or –ily if the adjective already ends in –y.

A) Change the following adjectives into adverbs. Compose a sentence for each.

	Adjective	Adverb		Adjective	Adverb
1.	calm	calmly	11.	noisy	_____
2.	warm	_____	12.	scarce	_____
3.	bitter	_____	13.	brave	_____
4.	fresh	_____	14.	cruel	_____
5.	final	_____	15.	loud	_____
6.	reckless	_____	16.	foolish	_____
7.	sweet	_____	17.	rapid	_____
8.	coward	_____	18.	patient	_____
9.	happy	_____	19.	wise	_____
10.	equal	_____	20.	heavy	_____

B) Write a suitable adverb and complete each sentence.
1. The prince spoke _____ to _____ .
2. The robber left _____ when _____ .
3. The goalkeeper _____ caught the ball and _____ .
4. We worked _____ until _____ .
5. The swallow flew _____ through _____ .
6. John's father shouted _____ when _____ .
7. The postman walked _____ along _____ .
8. Mary wept _____ because _____ .
9. The soldiers fought _____ but _____ .
10. The river flowed _____ towards _____ .

C) Write the opposite of the words in italics.
1. *Summer* days are *long* and *warm*.
2. The girl was *laughing* because she was *happy*.
3. The boy swam in the *shallow* pool.
4. The *wet* sand was *soft* under my feet.
5. *Late* one *evening* the swallows flew *southwards*.
6. The *old* lady walked along the *narrow* path.
7. The boy is *tall* and *fat*.
8. The aeroplane flew *above* the *white* clouds.

© Folens (not copiable)

Exercises

A) Hyphenated words

Join one word from each column to make ten hyphenated words. Write them in the middle column. Example: fire-escape.

1. safety	_____	deep
2. skipping	_____	house
3. fire	_____	hawk
4. search	_____	guard
5. knee	_____	beaten
6. sparrow	_____	escape
7. life	_____	fighter
8. weather	_____	rope
9. boat	_____	pin
10. fire	_____	party

B) New words: Anagrams

By rearranging the letters of the word on the left you will find the new word to fill the blank spaces.

slate   1. The policeman saw the robber **steal** the motor bicycle.

beard   2. The loaf of _____ was stale.

resist   3. My brother and _____ are twins.

last   4. John shook a pinch of _____ on the meat.

charm   5. The soldiers had to _____ in single file across the narrow bridge.

large   6. I was dazzled by the _____ of the sun's rays.

meats   7. The hissing _____ from the boiling kettle scalded my hand.

star   8. The hungry _____ ate the potatoes in the sack.

trades   9. She _____ softly across the room so as not to waken the young baby.

flit   10. The old lady was unable to _____ the heavy pot.

C) Missing words

Insert the missing word.

1. A pain in the tooth is called a t_____ .
2. A doctor who performs operations is called a s_____ .
3. A person who supplied spectacles is called an o_____ .
4. The breaking of a bone is called a f_____ .
5. A note given by a doctor for medicine is called a p_____ .
6. The long bone down the back is called the s_____ .
7. The instrument used to take your temperature is called a t_____ .
8. A person who dispenses medicine is called a ph_____ .
9. Operations are carried out in an operating t_____ .
10. The person treated by a doctor is called a p_____ .

© Folens (not copiable)

Idioms

Idioms and colloquialisms are common expressions used frequently in conversation. They have a meaning different from that which appears at first sight.

Examples:	**Explanations:**
1. All ears.	Listening attentively.
2. At loggerheads.	Not agreeing.
3. See eye to eye.	To agree with a person.
4. Turn a deaf ear.	Not to listen.
5. Fight tooth and nail.	To be very determined.
6. By the skin of one's teeth.	Barely, narrowly succeed.

A) Give the meaning of the following idioms:

1. Hang one's head. _____
2. To be tight-lipped. _____
3. Turn a blind eye. _____
4. Turn the other cheek. _____
5. Armed to the teeth. _____
6. To hold one's tongue. _____
7. To take forty winks. _____
8. To be cold-blooded. _____
9. Turn up one's nose. _____
10. Live from hand to mouth. _____
11. Throw dust in one's eyes. _____
12. Pull the wool over someone's eyes. _____
13. To keep a stiff upper lip. _____

Proverbs

A proverb is a wise saying which has been in use for hundreds of years.

A) Write in your own words what each of these proverbs means.

Let sleeping dogs lie.
Every cloud has a silver lining.
A good beginning is half the battle.
A stitch in time saves nine.
Every dog has its day.
Better late than never.
Out of sight, out of mind.
Birds of a feather flock together.
When in Rome, do as the Romans do.

To kill two birds with the one stone.
Practice makes perfect.
No news is good news.
A rolling stone gathers no moss.
Don't count your chickens before they are hatched.
The early bird catches the worm.
One swallow does not make a summer.

A visit to the dentist

A) Look carefully at these pictures. They tell the story of a visit to the dentist. The words and phrases help you to write the story.

Helpful words and phrases

throbbing toothache ...... cheeks puffed and swollen ...... waiting anxiously ...... smiling receptionist ...... friendly dentist ...... spotless white coat ...... big comfortable chair ...... gleaming overhead mirror ...... inspected my mouth ...... probed and prodded ...... needle pierced ...... gums as cold as ice ...... forceps ...... extraction ...... ugly decayed tooth ...... trickle of blood ...... sigh of relief ......

© Folens (not copiable)

The snow goose

Nell was disturbed at the thought of the man she had come so far to see, for she had heard frightening stories about him on her way to the lighthouse. Yet, she was anxious to see him, for she had been told by more than one person in this land of swamps that Meldon, the rough giant who was the chief keeper in the lighthouse, possessed a magic power of healing injured things. She knew, too, that the hunters hated him because he interfered with their sport, but even so, her fear was conquered by the hope in her childish heart that he would heal what she carried in her arms.

She had never seen Meldon, and all but fled in panic at the apparition which almost filled the doorway immediately she knocked – a huge man with jet-black head and beard, prominent hump and crooked, clawlike hand. She edged timidly forward and held out what she had been carrying – a large, white bird. There were blood stains on her frock and on the wings of the bird which lay quite still.

Meldon carried the bird into the house and gently placed it on a table where it moved feebly. Nell's curiosity drove her in and she found herself in a warm room with a bright coal fire. The walls were covered with coloured pictures, and there was a pleasant, if unusual, smell.

The bird fluttered slightly when Meldon, with his good hand, carefully opened out its immense, white wings. The man seemed puzzled and looked inquiringly at the child. "Where did you find this bird?" he asked. "In the marsh near our house, sir, where the hunters were shooting this morning. What is it ?"
"A snow goose from Canada."

A) Questions: Answer in sentences where possible.
1. Why was Nell disturbed?
2. How did Meldon interfere with the hunter's sport?
3. What helped Nell to overcome her fear?
4. Why did Nell edge 'timidly forward'?
5. How did the blood stains happen to be on Nell's frock?
6. Why did the bird remain so still?
7. Why was Nell so curious?
8. What do you think had happened to the bird?
9. Explain the following words: magic, apparition, prominent, fluttered, inquiringly.
10. Write each of the above words in a sentence of your own.

© Folens (not copiable)

Adjectives and adverbs

A) From the given nouns, find the adjectives and adverbs.

Nouns	Adjectives	Adverbs
1. patience	patient	patiently
2. vacancy	_____	_____
3. silence	_____	_____
4. kindness	_____	_____
5. intelligence	_____	_____
6. skill	_____	_____
7. quietness	_____	_____
8. happiness	_____	_____

B) Write in the most suitable adverb from the list given, and complete the sentence. (furiously, gracefully, powerfully, quietly, courageously, easily, bravely, swiftly, superbly, carefully.)

1. She skated _____ around _____ .
2. He sprinted _____ towards _____ .
3. John swam _____ through _____ .
4. The boxer fought _____ until _____ .
5. The referee walked _____ across _____ .
6. She played _____ for _____ .
7. Gary read _____ till _____ .
8. Emma was _____ the best _____ .
9. He wrestled _____ but _____ .
10. The driver drove _____ along _____ .

C) Choose a suitable adjective from the given list, and complete the sentence. (huge, agile, spotted, clumsy, timid, tiny, lean, majestic, cunning, frightened)

1. The _____ bear lumbered _____ .
2. The _____ leopard sprang _____ .
3. The _____ deer bounded _____ .
4. The _____ elephant ambled _____ .
5. The _____ lion prowled _____ .
6. The _____ monkey climbed _____ .
7. The _____ wolf loped _____ .
8. The _____ rabbit scurried _____ .
9. The _____ fox sneaked _____ .
10. The _____ mouse scampered _____ .

© Folens (not copiable)

Questions

A) Asking questions

Always begin a question with a capital letter and end it with a question mark. Write questions to which the following sentences are the answers. Use the words: When? Where? How? Why? Who? What?

1. The calf is two weeks old. _____
2. The young boy was badly injured. _____
3. The house is at the corner of the street. _____
4. I saw a flock of birds on the roof. _____
5. Because the house was on fire. _____
6. The old man went for a walk in the evening. _____
7. The runner ran twenty kilometres. _____
8. Colette danced gracefully. _____
9. I am feeling much better today. _____
10. It is seven o'clock. _____

B) Answering questions

In answering questions it is always best to write a full sentence.
Answer the following questions on the frog.

1. What is a young frog called? A young frog is a tadpole.
2. What are the eggs of the frog called? _____ .
3. When does the frog lay her eggs? _____ .
4. What sound does the frog make at night? _____ .
5. What enemies does the frog have? _____ .
6. What does a frog eat? _____ .
7. What colour is a frog? _____ .
8. Why is a frog a good swimmer? _____ .
9. Where do frogs go in winter? _____ .
10. Write six words that begin with fro– _____ .

'May' or 'can'

'May I' means 'Will you permit or allow me?'.
'May I borrow your car?' means 'Will you allow me to borrow your car?'
'Can I' means 'Am I able?'.
'Can you drive?' means 'Are you able to drive?'

C) In the following sentences insert 'may' or 'can' correctly.

1. _____ I study in the dining-room?
2. _____ you meet me tonight?
3. My father _____ bake beautiful cakes.
4. _____ I speak to the manager?
5. Mother, please _____ I have another slice of the cake?
6. You _____ go to the concert if you _____ pay for the ticket.
7. John says that he _____ teach me how to swim. _____ I go with him?

Exercises

A) From the clues given, find the right word. All the words have 'PH' sounded as 'F'.

1. The twenty six letters in the English language. a_____
2. A child who has no parents. o_____
3. The opposite of 'niece'. n_____
4. A school subject. g_____
5. A large animal with a trunk. e_____
6. An apparition or a ghost. p_____
7. What a camera takes. p_____
8. Another name for a record player. g_____
9. A common surname in Ireland. m_____
10. Victory. t_____
11. A wild bird with beautiful plumage. p_____
12. Doctor of medicine. p_____
13. A chemist's shop. p_____
14. A boy's name. p_____
15. A group of words. p_____

B) Insert the correct phrase in each sentence.
(again and again, above and beyond, spick and span, hand and foot, hammer and tongs, neck and neck, touch and go, wear and tear, here and there, odds and ends)

1. The basket contained an assortment of _____ .
2. Annette keeps her house _____ .
3. The two horses passed the winning post _____ .
4. The doctor said that it would be _____ if the patient lived.
5. He tired _____ until he succeeded.
6. The man's clothes were scattered _____ on the rocks.
7. Thomas received extra money for the _____ of his car.
8. She worked _____ to pass her examination.
9. The faithful maid waited _____ on her mistress.
10. The policeman risked his life _____ the call of duty.

C) Write the opposite of these words.

1. despair _____
2. occupied _____
3. invisible _____
4. retreat _____
5. innocent _____
6. praise _____
7. import _____
8. found _____
9. south _____
10. often _____
11. exit _____
12. admit _____

Write each new word in an interesting sentence of your own.

© Folens (not copiable)

Stories

A) Complete the following story.

Ann wriggled into the sack. She was trembling with excitement. However, she was determined to win the race. The starter raised his arm and cried, 'On your marks.'

B) Complete the following story.

It was Mary's first ride on 'Silver Spur'. She leapt with joy into the saddle. A gentle touch of the reins, a word of encouragement, and horse and rider cantered across the field.

C) Complete the following story.

Last Saturday my friends and I went swimming in the 'Black Pool'. We had tremendous fun in the cool water. Suddenly a cry for help rent the air. I rushed to the bank.

D) Complete the following story.

"See how fast I can go", cried Pat, as he raced past his admiring friends. He sped recklessly down the street. Daringly, he circled the roundabout. Suddenly ......

The Titanic

Containing eleven decks and stretching a full 305 metres, she was the greatest ocean liner of her time. This ship had been fitted out in true style, with plush cabins, electric lifts, squash courts, gymnasium and a heated indoor swimming pool. There was a hospital to cope with any passengers who became ill; and to cater for meals, she carried a dinner service of 100,000 plates. The owners, the shipbuilders, the captain – in fact, everyone – said the *Titanic* was unsinkable. Perhaps this was the reason why only enough lifeboats for half of the passengers were placed on board. Tickets for her maiden voyage were snapped up eagerly, and there were over 2,000 people on board when she set out from Southampton for New York on April 11th 1912.

Disaster was to strike after only four days at sea. With a captain and crew determined to break the record for an Atlantic crossing, the liner had been ploughing through calm, glass-like seas at a speed of 22 knots. She had entered an area known as the Grand Banks when radio reports from other ships were received, warning of icebergs. The warnings were ignored. The *Titanic* steamed ahead at full speed. It was almost midnight when Frederick Fleet, the look-out in the crow's nest, suddenly spotted an iceberg looming ahead in the darkness. But, his frantic warning cries were too late to prevent the collision. A huge hole was ripped into the side of the liner and the water poured in.

At first, the passengers treated the incident as a joke; yet, within ten minutes, the water had risen five metres inside the ship. Distress signals were sent out to the nearby liner, *California*, but her radio had unfortunately been switched off. Panic now spread, as the huge liner listed to one side and began to sink. By the time another liner, *Carpathia*, finally arrived to help, fifteen hundred people had drowned in the icy seas. The loss of the *Titanic* was one of the greatest catastrophes in the history of navigation.

A) Questions: Answer in sentences where possible.
1. What major safety error did the builders of the *Titanic* make?
2. Why was such a basic error allowed to occur?
3. Describe the *Titanic*.
4. What was the destination of her maiden voyage?
5. What blunder did the captain make?
6. Why did Frederick Fleet become alarmed?
7. Why did the *Califomian* not come to help the stricken liner?
8. How many people drowned?
9. Pretend you are a newspaper reporter in 1912. Write a paragraph telling about the loss of the *Titanic*.
10. Find out the meaning of: plush, frantic, looming, incident, listed.
11. Write each of the above words in a sentence of your own.

   © Folens (not copiable)

Abbreviations

Sometimes words are not written in full. We often shorten or abbreviate them.

Examples: a) Captain John Fogarty   Capt J Fogarty

              b) Doctor Nora Mary White   Dr N M White

              c) Reverend Terence Connolly   Rev T Connolly

Remember: Initials are written in capital letters.

A) Rewrite the following in abbreviated form. The first one is given.

Months	Abbreviations	Days	Abbreviations
January	Jan	Sunday	Sun
February	_____	Monday	_____
March	_____	Tuesday	_____
April	_____	Wednesday	_____
August	_____	Thursday	_____
September	_____	Friday	_____
October	_____	Saturday	_____
November	_____		
December	_____		

Note: The days and months of the year are written with capital letters. There are no abbreviations for May, June, July.

B) Rewrite the following sentences. Insert capital letters where necessary.
1. Next week a lecture will be given by Prof m b Farley.
2. Liz Smith and t Browne will present the new television show.
3. Fr p h Green sat next to Mrs h Mooney.
4. Dr m l Clarke visited Capt ray Byrne.
5. Mr w s Fitzwilliam is our headmaster.
6. Yesterday, mrs k O'Neill died at 6 a.m.
7. My best friends are e McCarthy and j Murphy.
8. Lt Collins and Sgt Lynch went on the climbing expedition.
9. Next wed, Brown and co Ltd are going to open a new supermarket.
10. Mrs b Stokes works near St john's Hospital.

CAPT   Tues

Dr   PROF

Mrs   Mon

FRI   WEd

E.E.C   G.P.O.

C) Write the following in abbreviated form.
1. General Post Office.
2. United Nations Organisation.
3. European Union.
4. United States of America.
5. Federal Bureau of Investigation.
6. Trans-World Airways.
7. Confederation of Independent States.
8. British Broadcasting Corporation.

Homonyms

Homonyms are words that are pronounced alike but differ in meaning.

A) Choose the correct word from those in the margin to fill in the blank spaces. Write the sentences.

blue, blew   1. The wind _____ away her _____ hat.

threw, through 2. He _____ the ball right _____ the window.

herd, heard   3. I _____ the lowing of the _____ in the field.

bare, bear   4. The huge _____ disappeared behind the _____ rock.

week, weak   5. The girl was so feeble and _____ that she could not attend the concert last _____ .

pane, pain   6. She cut her hand on the _____ of glass and it caused her great _____ .

heal, heel   7. The boy injured his _____ and it took a long time to _____ .

ball, bawl   8. The young girl began to _____ when the big _____ struck her on the nose.

B) Which is which?
1. air, heir, Ayr.   Which is the town in Scotland? _____
2. you, ewe, yew.   Which is a female sheep? _____
3. scent, sent, cent.   Which is a coin? _____
4. palate, pallet, palette. Which is a painter's board? _____
5. so, sow, sew.   Which means 'to scatter'? _____
6. i'll, isle, aisle.   Which is an island? _____
7. too, to, two.   Which is twice one? _____
8. seas, seize, sees.   Which means 'to grasp'? _____
9. vale, veil, vail.   Which is a valley? _____
10. raise, rays, raze.   Which are beams of light? _____
11. rain, rein, reign.   Which is part of a horse's bridle? _____
12. meet, meat, mete. Which is food? _____
13. heel, heal, he'll.   Which is the back part of the foot? _____
14. idle, idol, idyll.   Which is a false god? _____
15. cite, site, sight.   Which means 'to summon'? _____
16. pare, pair, pear. Which means a 'couple'? _____

C) Write what each homonym means. (Use a dictionary if necessary.)

1. Ate Eight	5. Dew Due	9. Key Quay
2. Deer Dear	6. Feet Feat	10. Leek Leak
3. Beech Beach	7. Foul Fowl	11. New Knew
4. Bow Bough	8. Hale Hail	12. Our Hour

© Folens (not copiable)

The apostrophe (')

When we want to show that something belongs to someone, we use an apostrophe.
Examples:
Singular
1. The girl's scissors means the scissors of the girl.
2. The bird's egg means the egg of the bird.

Plural
The girls' scissors means the scissors of the girls.
The birds' eggs means the eggs of the birds.

A) Insert the apostrophes where they are needed in the following sentences.
1. Veronicas hat is in the monkeys cage.
2. She took my friends pen from the teachers desk.
3. Mrs Smiths car is parked in West Street.
4. I found the postmans hat on the road.
5. The pupils magazine was in tatters.
6. The boys fishing hook got caught in Michaels scarf.
7. I borrowed my neighbours tractor.
8. Seans trousers were sent for repairs.
9. The boys coat was floating in the pond.

Exceptions

When the plural of the noun does not end in s, we add 's.
Examples:
1. The men's hats means the hats of the men.
2. The children's toys means the toys of the children.
3. The women's glasses means the glasses of the women.

'Its' or 'it's'

'**its**' means 'belonging to something'. For example, 'the dog's eyes are swollen and its nose is bleeding'.

'**it's**' means 'it is' or 'it has'. For example, 'it's a pity it's not a fine day. It's been snowing heavily'.

B) Fill in the blank spaces in the following sentences with either 'it's' or 'its'.
1. _____ not clear if _____ back is broken.
2. The soup has lost _____ flavour.
3. The peacock is proud of _____ feathers.
4. The swallow returned to _____ nest.
5. _____ a shame that _____ fur is torn.
6. _____ shell protects it from _____ enemies.
7. The horse tossed _____ head in the air and rolled over on _____ side.

© Folens (not copiable)

Quotation marks

When writing the above sentences, only the words spoken are written inside the quotation marks.

Examples: a) "I think those, dark clouds are a sign of rain," said Peter.
b) Mary says, "He is a fantastic pop-singer."
c) "Who is the camp leader?" asked Anna.

A) Write out the following sentences correctly. Where needed, put in the quotations marks, capital letter, commas and question marks.
1. The conductor announced the bus is full.
2. Helen said I dislike going to the dentist.
3. The farmer shouted close the gate after you.
4. Sally whispered it is hidden underneath the stone.
5. The doctor asked did you ever have the measles.
6. Ann enquired where is the new museum.
7. Jimmy asked when are we getting our holidays.
8. You have broken my new pen sobbed Mark.
9. I am the best footballer boasted Harry.
10. When did you arrive enquired mother.
11. May I borrow your English book requested Dick.
12. Who scored the last goal asked Ruth.
13. Have you any old shoes asked the beggar.
14. The inspector asked who can recite the poem.
15. Mrs Kelly remarked my daughter has passed the examination.
16. Tom shouted don't go without me.

© Folens (not copiable)

Conversation

A) You left a new coat in the bus. Imagine the conversation you would have with the clerk in the Lost Property Office.

Clerk: Hello! this is the Lost Property Office.

You: _____

Clerk: What was the number of the bus you were travelling on?

You: _____

Clerk: Where were you sitting in the bus?

You: _____

Clerk: Please give me a description of the coat.

You: _____

Clerk: Did you have anything in the pockets?

You: _____

Clerk: Yes, we have a coat here that fits that description. You may collect it any day between 9.00a.m. and 6.00p.m.

You: _____

B) Manners and politeness

What do you say when:

1. You receive a gift? _____
2. You are introduced to a person? _____
3. You awkwardly stand on a person's foot? _____
4. You meet an old friend in the street? _____
5. You ask for directions? _____
6. You go to a birthday party? _____
7. You apologise for doing something wrong? _____
8. You contradict a person? _____
9. Your uncle and aunt visit your house? _____
10. Your friend passes her examination? _____

C) Complete the following telephone conversation.

Duncan: Hello, may I speak to Deirdre, please?

Deidre: _____

Duncan: Hello Deirdre! This is Duncan speaking.

Deirdre: _____

Duncan: Our class is going on a cycling tour to Windermere next Sunday. Perhaps you would like to join us?

Deidre: _____

Duncan: Fine! I shall expect to meet you outside the Town Hall at nine o'clock.

Deidre: _____

© Folens (not copiable)

The Stone Age

A) Imagine you are living in the Stone Age. Describe an exciting hunting expedition in which you took part.

Helpful information

1. Home

large cave dwelling ...... many families ...... near a babbling stream ...... dug-out canoes for fishing ...... sharp flint spears and arrowheads ...... dense forests ...... deer ...... wild boars ......

2. Hunt

hunting expedition ...... departed at sunrise ...... flint arrowheads ...... spears ...... dogs ...... stalked the animal ...... the chase ...... deer bounded over rocks ...... trapped at the edge of a cliff ...... shower of arrows and spears ...... fell mortally wounded ...... gigantic elk ...... the carcass ...... homeward trip ......

3. Feast

blazing fire ...... roasted the meat on a spit ...... women busy ...... crackling of wood ...... story of the hunt retold ...... the hunting scene painted on the cave walls ...... paint from soot and crushed clay mixed with animal fat ...... paint brushes from animal hair ......scraped the fat from the animal's hide ...... softened the hide by chewing it ...... clothes made from it ......animal sinews used as thread ...... bone needles ...... tools and weapons ...... antlers used as pickaxes ...... necklaces and bracelets from the teeth of the animals ......

© Folens (not copiable)

Wonders of the universe

Most astronomers agree that our galaxy, known as The Milky Way, contains roughly 180,000 million other suns as well as that sun which shines over our earth each day. They have calculated that light, which travels at the incredible speed of 299,796 kilometres per second, will take 4 Qe years to reach us from the nearest sun and 80,000 years from the furthest sun in one galaxy. Even more mind-boggling is the fact that there exists about 80,000 million other galaxies in the great Universe!

It is not just the vastness of the universe that can leave us gasping with astonishment. Not so long ago, scientists were flabbergasted to find out that there are black holes in space. Such a discovery seemed to belong more to the world of science fiction than to that of science fact. Yet black holes were real. How could they be explained? It seems that some stars are so massive that they begin to collapse under their own weight. As the star crushes itself, it gets dimmer and dimmer, and its material becomes very dense and very heavy. A star that condenses itself down to about the size of the earth is known as a White Dwarf. A teaspoon of material from it would weigh about five tonnes! Other stars – known as Neutron Stars – have condensed even more, so that they may be only 16 kilometres wide. A teaspoon of material from one would weigh 100 million tonnes!

But, some stars collapse completely into nothing: a black hole is left. It is believed that these holes spin round at the stupendous speed of 1,000 times per second. Any object that fell into a black hole would be torn into a billion pieces. Our galaxy alone may contain millions of these amazing black holes.

A) Questions: Answer in sentences where possible.
1. What is The Milky Way?
2. How fast does light travel?
3. How many galaxies are there in the universe?
4. Why were scientists flabbergasted?
5. What can happen to some of the biggest stars?
6. What is a Neutron Star?
7. When is a black hole created?
8. Write a short story about an imaginary space voyage to a black hole.
9. There are nine planets in our solar system. Can you name them?
10. Find out the meaning of these words: flabbergasted, fiction, dense, condense, stupendous.
11. Write each of the above words in a sentence of your own.

© Folens (not copiable)

Similes

A simile is a figure of speech comparing two unlike things and is often introduced by 'like' or 'as'.

A) Complete the following similes.

1. The boy was as hungry as a _____ .
2. The prisoner was as stubborn as a _____ .
3. The small girl was as meek as a _____ .
4. The baby was as playful as a _____ .
5. The suitcase was as light as a _____ .
6. Her cheeks were as red as a _____ .
7. The farmer was as strong as a _____ .
8. The servant was as cunning as a _____ .
9. The old man was as wise as an _____ .
10. The young boy was as sick as a _____ .

B) Use these similes to make interesting sentences.

1. As pale as death.
2. As quick as lightening.
3. As clean as a new pin.
4. As clear as crystal.
5. As silent as the grave.
6. As white as a sheet.
7. As busy as an ant.
8. As brown as a berry.
9. As soft as putty.
10. As old as the hills.
11. As fast as a hare.
12. As black as coal.
13. As heavy as lead.
14. As fresh as a daisy.
15. As swift as a deer.
16. As graceful as a swan.
17. As poor as a church mouse.
18. As weak as water.

C) Complete the following:

1. The seal was as black as _____ .
2. The acrobat has a face as round as an _____ .
3. The clown saw the ball coming and he ducked as quickly as _____ .
4. Mary blushed and her cheeks became as red as a _____ .
5. The winner was as proud as _____ .
6. He wore glasses because he was as blind as a _____ .
7. The twins were as like as two _____ .
8. Her cheeks were as cold as _____ .
9. His face was as white as a _____ .
10. The teacher is nearly as tall as _____ .

70

© Folens (not copiable)

Participles

The past participle requires another verb with it, the verb 'to be' or 'to have'.
Examples: a) He has gone; b) She was kept busy; c) We were awakened.

A) Examine the following verbs and compose a sentence for each form of the verb
  – present, past and past participle.

Present	Past	Past participle
1. awake	awoke	awakened
2. arise	arose	arisen
3. beat	beat	beaten
4. blow	blew	blown
5. begin	began	begun
6. choose	chose	chosen
7. bite	bit	bitten
8. come	came	come

B) Fill in the past and past participle form of each verb.

Present	Past	Past participle
1. give	gave	given
2. go	_____	_____
3. hold	_____	_____
4. know	_____	_____
5. ring	_____	_____
6. rise	_____	_____
7. sing	_____	_____
8. speak	_____	_____
9. stand	_____	_____
10. steal	_____	_____

C) Underline the correct form of the verb in brackets.
1. He has just (wrote, written) to his cousin to ask him if he had (took, taken) the book.
2. After he had (sang, sung) the song, I (spoke, spoken) to him.
3. If I had (rang, rung) the bell she would have (awoke, wakened) in time.
4. Before I had (ate, eaten) my dinner I went and (swam, swum) in the lake.
5. The coat which he (wom, wore) has been (stole, stolen).
6. He had (took, taken) the day off because he (is, was) sick.
7. The gardener (stood, stand) near the hole he had (dug, dig).
8. The whistle was (blown, blew) and the game (began, begun).
9. The mother cried because she (knew, know) that her son had (did, done) the robbery.
10. When he had (drew, drawn) the picture he (gave, give) it to the lady.
11. Although he had (went, gone) home late, he had not (seen, saw) the crime committed.
12. I (began, begin) to wonder if he had (fell, fallen) into the water.
13. After the boy had (threw, thrown) the stone he (ran, run) away.
14. Yesterday when the teacher (come, came) into the room the pupils (stand, stood).
15. After he had (wrote, written) the letter he was (took, taken) to jail.

© Folens (not copiable)

A word game

A) Changing words.
Change the word 'pig' into 'cat' in three moves by changing one letter each time.
For example:

pig   ⟶   pi**T** ➤ p**A**t ➤ **C**at

Do the following ones:

lot	_____ _____	him	
dog	_____ _____	cat	
net	_____ _____	dog	

bin	_____ _____	leg	
cow	_____ _____	jam	
van	_____ _____	pig	

B) Words pronounced alike, but differing in meaning. Examine the clues and then write down the words.

1. Contraction of 'are not' _aren't____

   A close relation _aunt_____

2. A male child _____

   A floating sign for ships _____

3. A female horse _____

   A head of a town _____

4. A bag of postal letters _____

   The opposite of female _____

5. A female sheep _____

   An evergreen tree _____

6. A strong odour _____

   An American coin _____

7. A valley _____

   A covering for the face _____

8. Used in a game _____

   To cry loudly _____

9. A male pig _____

   To make a hole _____

10. A branch of a tree _____

    Part of a ship _____

C) Compose eight words that include the letters in the words given. The first word is done for you.

cat	catalogue	_____
air	chair	_____
ale	stale	_____
ear	rear	_____
lip	tulip	_____
ate	crate	_____
ore	core	_____

© Folens (not copiable)

A kind deed

A) Write an essay based on the pictures underneath.

Helpful words and phrases

pitter-patter of rain ...... puddles of water ......
windswept streets ...... gusts of wind ......
people hurrying home ...... umbrella turned
inside-out ...... to the rescue ...... invitation
...... chatted ...... sipped hot cups of tea ......
storm raged ...... flashed of lightning ......
peals of thunder ...... torrential rain ......

© Folens (not copiable)

Volcanoes

Far beneath the surface of the earth, where the pressure is enormous, so great is the heat that the rock itself has melted. This molten rock forms a layer 1,800 kilometres deep, and every so often the pressure squeezes it out through weak points on the earth's surface. An eruption of molten rock from the earth is called a volcano. The ancient Romans believe a volcanoes to be the work of Vulcan, their god of fire, hence the origin of the name volcano. Romans had good reason to fear them, for in 79 A.D. the town of Pompeii, with a population of 20,000, was entirely destroyed by the volcanic eruption of the mountain of Vesuvius. Vesuvius is one of 800 volcanoes still active in the world today.

The awesome destructive power of the volcano was felt all over the world on August 27th 1883, when one of the greatest eruptions in human history took place. It happened in Krakatoa, an island of about 24 square kilometres in size, in the Sundra Strait near Indonesia. It was a gigantic explosion – scientists estimate it was as powerful as twenty-five atomic bombs. So loud was the eruption, it was clearly heard over 5,000 kilometres away; so intense were the shock waves produced that they circled the entire globe twice. Nearly two-thirds of the island was blown to pieces, as rocks and ashes were hurled 30 kilometres into the sky. It is believed that the vast dust cloud formed as a result, caused the temperature of the world to drop by two degrees.

It was also a terrible human disaster: the explosion set off giant waves, 30 metres high, that swept away 150 villages, killing over 36,000 people. The only living thing on the island to survive was a tiny monkey, which was found clinging to a piece of wood in the sea. Although badly burned, it was restored to full health by the kind sailors who rescued it.

A) Questions: Answer in sentences where possible.
1. What is a volcano?
2. What happened to the town of Pompeii in the year 79 A.D. ?
3. Where does the name volcano come from?
4. What happened on August 27th, 1883?
5. How powerful was the explosion at Krakatoa?
6. In what way did this volcanic eruption affect the world's weather?
7. Can you guess how the huge dust cloud had the described weather effect?
8. Did any living thing survive on Krakatoa?
9. Can you guess what a vulcanologist studies?
10. Find out the meaning of these words: awesome, intense, restored, eruption, molten.
11. Write each of the above words in a sentence of your own.

© Folens (not copiable)

Tenses

A) Past tense
Write the verbs in the past tense.
1. I think I see the postman coming down the road.
2. I buy stamps in the Post Office when I go there.
3. I write often to my friend who lives in Stoke.
4. I collect and deliver the mail at Christmas time.
5. My father drives the train because that is his job.
6. I swim in the lake when the weather is fine.
7. I help my mother when I am on holidays.
8. The old sailor rings the bell and blows the horn whenever there is fog.
9. Every time I hear a knock I expect to see the postman at the door.
10. The man words as a clerk and sells stamps to the customers.

B) Present tense
The verbs in brackets are in the singular form. Re-write them in the present tense.
1. Each of the dolls (*to have*) a red nose.
2. Neither of the monkeys (*to go*) into the cage.
3. One of the acrobats (*to be*) injured.
4. Every man (*to know*) what to do.
5. Nobody (*to wish*) to see the man fall.
6. Every one of us (*to like*) to go to the circus.
7. Not one of the girls (*to have*) a ticket.
8. Each of the dogs (*to be*) sick.
9. Each child (*to receive*) a present.
10. Everybody (*to be*) delighted with the child's progress.

C) Future tense
Rewrite in the future tense.
1. I saw him yesterday.
2. The last time I met her, she was very busy.
3. We gathered the sheep and went to the fair.
4. He brought his son to Hyde Park on Sunday.
5. I came, I saw, I conquered.
6. I caught a salmon in the Tweed last month.

Dictionary practice

These words are spelt and pronounced alike, but differ in meaning.
Example: Bat – an animal with wings.
           Bat – a club to strike a ball.

A) Give at least two meanings for each word. (Use a dictionary to help you if necessary.)

bill	game	date
bat	grave	draw
blade	hail	crane
box	scale	club
corn	spring	comb
court	perch	sound
crow	palm	set
flag	nail	graze

B) The words in the following list are often confused. Use your dictionary to help you write out their different meanings. Then, make up sentences to show the differences between the words.

1. accept _____
   except _____
2. adapt _____
   adopt _____
3. allowed _____
   aloud _____
4. astrology _____
   astronomy _____
5. bare _____
   bear _____
6. board _____
   bored _____
7. brake _____
   break _____
8. broach _____
   brooch _____
9. check _____
   cheque _____
10. desert _____
    dessert _____
11. detract _____
    distract _____
12. discover _____
    invent _____
13. dual _____
    duel _____
14. emigrant _____
    immigrant _____

15. ensure _____
    insure _____
16. envelop _____
    envelope _____
17. faint _____
    feint _____
18. flaunt _____
    flout _____
19. hoard _____
    horde _____
20. idle _____
    idol _____
21. larva _____
    lava _____
22. lead _____
    led _____
23. loose _____
    lose _____
24. peace _____
    piece _____
25. persecute _____
    prosecute _____
26. plain _____
    plane _____
27. prey _____
    pray _____

28. proceed _____
    precede _____
29. quiet _____
    quite _____
30. rain _____
    reign _____
31. scarce _____
    rare _____
32. sensitive _____
    sensible _____
33. sow _____
    sew _____
34. shear _____
    sheer _____
35. sight _____
    site _____
36. taut _____
    taught _____
37. waist _____
    waste _____
38. weather _____
    whether _____
39. would _____
    wood _____
40. you're _____
    your _____

© Folens (not copiable)

Occupations

A) From the list of occupations in brackets choose a suitable one for each boy and girl. Read the clues carefully.

(footballer, actor, pilot, cook, artist, florist, jockey, soldier, hairdresser, doctor.)

1. Paul likes cooking and baking fruit cakes. Paul would like to be a _____ .
2. David is keen and eager to play games.
3. Anne hopes to fly around the world.
4. Michael hopes to join the army.
5. Jack likes acting in the school play.
6. Joan hopes to work in a hospital.
7. Olive enjoys arranging flowers.
8. Catherine likes to cut and style hair.
9. David enjoys riding horses.
10. John paints beautiful pictures.

B) Who am I?

Choose your answer from the list below.

(optician, coroner, journalist, pharmacist, sculptor, detective, judge.)

1. I write articles for newspapers and magazines. _____

2. I chisel and carve figures. _____

3. I look after people's eyes and prescribe glasses. _____

4. I investigate special crimes. _____

5. I have the authority to administer the law. _____

6. I am the legal person appointed to discover
   the cause of unusual deaths. _____

7. I dispense medical prescriptions. _____

C) Imagine you are the newsreader on television. Begin like this:
Today is Thursday, the 22nd of September. Here are the news headlines.

_____
_____
_____
_____
_____
_____
_____
_____
_____
_____
_____

The signs of spring

A) Write an essay describing the joys of spring.

Sun
Lengthening days ...... softening winds ......
gentle showers ...... mother earth awakens ......

Growth
green shoots ...... blossoming trees ...... shooting
buds ...... blooming flowers ...... pretty
snowdrops...... golden daffodils.

Birds

birds nesting ...... chorus of song ...... the
cuckoo's arrival ...... hungry young birds ......
feeding time ......

Farmer
Busy season ...... ploughing ...... harrowing ......
sowing the seed ...... caring for young lambs ......

© Folens (not copiable)

The conquest of space

On the 12th of April 1961, Flight Major Yuri Gagarin became the first person in space when he orbited the earth in his spacecraft, Vostok I, at a height of 300 kilometres, for an hour and forty-eight minutes. Gagarin became a legend overnight. Quite forgotten now is the tiny female dog named Laika, that four years earlier had the distinction of being the first living creature to orbit earth and had played a vital role in paving the way for later space flights by humans. In fact, the quest to conquer space had started as far back as 1949, when the Russians and Americans earnestly began to grapple with the problems involved. The problems they faced were daunting. It was simply not possible to use aircraft or balloons to venture into space because these relied on air to support them, and space was a vacuum, without air. Also, in order to escape from the massive downward pull of the earth due to gravity, it was obvious that what was needed was a totally new vehicle of great power and speed.

To overcome these problems, scientists turned to a thousand year old Chinese invention, the rocket. Rockets work in much the same way as any ordinary balloon. When its air is allowed to rush out, it shoots forward. Rockets must burn fuel extremely quickly, so that enough hot gases can be released to shoot the rocket forward into the atmosphere. Unless a rocket can reach – within minutes of lift-off – a speed greater than 29,000 kilometres per hour, it will not escape from the earth's pull. This speed is called the earth's escape velocity.

Once 'escape' from the earth has been achieved, only very small rocket-power is needed to orbit in space. It takes a spacecraft such as the space shuttle only 90 minutes to orbit earth. During this time, the astronauts will spend 45 minutes in bright daylight on one side of the earth and 45 minutes in darkness on the other. In the darkness, the astronauts can clearly see the city lights shining below; while in daylight, the only man-made structure they can make out is the Great Wall of China. The Chinese, it seem, were great builders as well as great inventors.

A) Questions: Answer in sentences where possible.
1. Who was Yuri Gagarin?
2. What distinction in space history is owed to a dog?
3. What two countries were involved in the 'space race'?
4. Why is it so difficult to go from earth into outer space?
5. Explain how a rocket works?
6. Who invented the rocket?
7. What does the term 'escape velocity' mean?
8. How long does it take to orbit the earth?
9. Write the names of the nine planets in our solar system, and any constellations of stars you know.
10. Find out the meaning of: orbit, distinction, vacuum, grapple, earnest, daunting.
11. Write each of the above words in a sentence of your own.

Prefix and suffix

Prefix

A prefix is a group of letters added to the beginning of a word to give a new word.

A) Add un– to the beginning of the following words and write a sentence for each.

1. willing	4. reliable	7. cover
2. known	5. beaten	8. lock
3. kind	6. fair	9. true

un fore re **fore** re
inter *in* **mis** *in* un *in*

B) Write one of the following prefixes for each of the words below: re–, un–, mis–, inter–, in–, fore–.

1. _____ national	6. _____ usual	11. _____ arrange
2. _____ build	7. _____ gone	12. _____ mix
3. _____ cast	8. _____ side	13. _____ name
4. _____ human	9. _____ judge	14. _____ match
5. _____ take	10. _____ roll	15. _____ tell

Suffix

A suffix is a group of letters added to the end of a word to give a new word.

A) Add –less to the end of the following words and write a sentence for each.

1. care	4. spot	7. end
2. cloud	5. tooth	8. pain
3. taste	6. home	9. luck

OUS *able* *ful* **able** ful **ous** *able* **ous** **ful**

B) Write five words for each suffix.

–able	–ous	–ful
1. _____	_____	_____
2. _____	_____	_____
3. _____	_____	_____
4. _____	_____	_____
5. _____	_____	_____

© Folens (not copiable)

Fun with words

A) Find the missing letters from the clues give.

1. _ oo _ A silly person.
2. _ oo _ Midday.
3. _ oo _ The opposite of 'rich'.
4. _ oo _ Worn by a sheep.
5. _ oo _ Dirt from the chimney.
6. _ oo _ It shines at night.
7. _ oo _ Stolen goods.
8. _ oo _ A hen's house.
9. _ oo _ Worn on the foot.
10. _ oo _ He prepares meals.
11. _ oo _ A place for swimming.
12. _ oo _ Part of a plant under the ground.

B) Find the missing letters from the clues given.

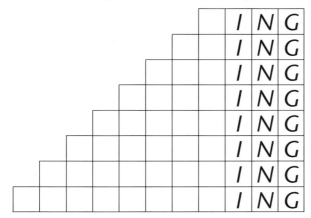

	I	N	G	Worn on the finger.
I	N	G		The defence a bee has.
I	N	G		One of the seasons.
I	N	G		Moving on ice.
I	N	G		A work produced by an artist.
I	N	G		Preparing the soil for seed.
I	N	G		Speaking in a very low voice.
I	N	G		The opposite of forgetting.

C) Each of these 'triangular words' starts at the top with one letter or a small word. Each line below has a letter added, either at the beginning or at the end, to make another word. Try and find at least four words.

Examples: Finish these ones:

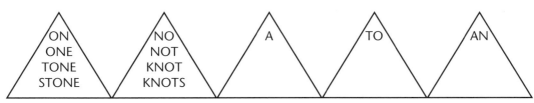

```
    ON          NO           A          TO          AN
   ONE         NOT
   TONE        KNOT
   STONE       KNOTS
```

D) Find the missing letters from the clues given.

1. _ oa _ A score.
2. _ oa _ Used for fishing.
3. _ oa _ Article of clothing.
4. _ oa _ A wild pig.
5. _ oa _ A young horse.
6. _ oa _ A loud shout.
7. _ oa _ Used for washing.
8. _ oa _ Bread.
9. _ oa _ To lend.
10. _ oa _ Black substance dug out of the earth.

The importance of words

A) Write down words similar in meaning to the words below.

1. find _____
2. scared _____
3. buy _____
4. hide _____

5. lift _____
6. shove _____
7. mend _____
8. vanish _____

9. copy _____
10. scent _____
11. feeble _____
12. yearly _____

B) What do we call:

1. A place where bees are kept? _____
2. A place where cars are kept? _____
3. A place where aeroplanes are kept? _____
4. A place where wine bottles are kept? _____
5. A place where tomatoes grow? _____
6. A place where grapes grow? _____
7. A place where books are kept? _____
8. A place where tea grows? _____
9. A place where apples grow? _____
10. A place where oranges grow? _____

C) In the following sentences give one word for each group of words in italics.
Examples: In the garage smoking was *not allowed*.   *Prohibited.*

1. The school concert is held *once every year*.   a_____
2. In winter the frog goes *for a long rest*.   h_____
3. The game was *put off* until next week.   p_____
4. We must leave *at once* if we are to catch the school bus.   i_____
5. Every year the swallows *fly from one country to another*.   m_____
6. *Over and over again* he played the same tune.   r_____
7. The explorer told a story about *savages who ate human flesh*.   c_____
8. I consulted the *list of books* in the library.   c_____
9. The flowers were *not real but made of plastic*.   a_____
10. He wrote his *life story*.   a_____

D) The following words are used in America. Write the word that would be used in Britain.

1. candy _____
2. movie _____
3. cookies _____

4. sidewalk _____
5. elevator _____
6. ice box _____

7. automobile _____
8. gasoline _____
9. schedule _____

        © Folens (not copiable)

A treasury of words

A) In the list below underline the words that give another word when spelt backwards. For example: tap = pat, door = rood.
(ship, nib, cat, top, bed, now, ten, cup, was, ton, pod, cool, room, reed, loop, loot, heel, leer, live, peels, moth, rail, gold, corn, draw)

B) In the following give one word meaning the same as, and one meaning the opposite. The first word is completed for you.

Word	Same	Opposite
rich	wealthy	poor
kind	_____	_____
fat	_____	_____
bitter	_____	_____
meek	_____	_____
round	_____	_____
end	_____	_____
hard	_____	_____
courageous	_____	_____
permit	_____	_____

C) Descriptive words.
Group the following words under their correct headings.
(cross, lonesome, frightened, jolly, sorrowful, happy, scared, cheerful, annoyed, miserable, furious, joyful, terrified, gloomy, vexed, apprehensive)

Fear	Happiness	Anger	Sadness
1. _____	_____	_____	_____
2. _____	_____	_____	_____
3. _____	_____	_____	_____
4. _____	_____	_____	_____

D) Underline the most suitable word in brackets.
1. The (*big, great, tiny*) dwarf in the circus made the children laugh.
2. A (*tiny, huge, little*) giant of a man stepped into the ring.
3. A (*small, great, enormous*) baby crawled into the caravan.
4. The (*tall, large, little*) giraffe ate all the bananas.
5. The strong man bent a (*large, tiny, small*) iron bar.
6. The (*big, tall, little*) lamb was just born.
7. The ship struck a (*great, small, tiny*) rock and sank.
8. The (*little, big, small*) elephant thundered around the ring.

© Folens (not copiable)

The first trout

A) The first paragraph is written. Finish this essay.

1. It was my first day fishing. Dad selected his favourite fishing spot on the river. I watched anxiously as he attached the wriggling worm to the hook. With a flick of the wrist, he skilfully landed the bait in the middle of the river.

2. Clutched the rod ...... cast out into the swirling waters ...... landed the hook among the reeds and rushes ...... entangled ...... difficulty in freeing it ...... finally succeeded ...... tempted to give up fishing ...... encouraged by Dad to persevere ......

3. Felt a tug on the line ...... thrill of delight ...... trembling with excitement ...... nearly fell into the river ...... the speckled trout leaped out of the water ...... reeled in the line ...... rod bending with the weight ...... the fishing-net ...... size of fish ...... weight ...... continued fishing ...... homeward trip with your catch.

4. Gave a detailed description of a day's fishing ...... stories about the fish that escaped ...... delicious supper of fresh fried or grilled trout ...... planned another trip ......

84

© Folens (not copiable)

The story of the computer

We think of the computer as the most modern of modern inventions, yet the ideas that led to computers can be traced as far back as 3,000 B.C. with the invention of the abacus. The abacus was an ancient mathematical devise consisting of beads strung on wires to represent units, tens, hundreds and so on. Using the abacus it was possible to do very quick adding calculations involving 'carrying', and this 'carrying' is a key aspect of electronic computers today. Yet it was not until 1830 before the next giant leap towards the computer occurred. Charles Babbage, who is now recognised as the 'father of computers', produced an amazing machine which had all the essential parts of a modern computer. Maths problems could be fed on cards into one side of the machine and the answers could be printed out on the other. Unfortunately for this genius, his machine was a huge unwieldy mass of connecting levers and gears and was simply too difficult to work. Babbage was too far ahead of his time.

But with the new invention of electricity anything became possible. It was more than a century later when Babbage's idea of a machine that could be programmed with a whole range of tasks was finally realised. The world's first electronic computer, the Mark I, was a massive breakthrough in that moving mechanical parts were replaced by electric wire and numbers were replaced in a new form by electronic signals moving at the speed of light! Weighing many tons, the Mark I stood as tall as a single-deck bus and was twice as long; it contained hundreds of miles of wiring and clicked incessantly as it worked out calculations at the rate of 5,000 per second. Since its arrival in 1943 the progress of the computer has been breathtaking. Today there are computers capable of 200,000 operations per second which are no bigger than a small TV set. And there are almost a hundred super-computers in existence capable of several hundred million operations per second. Breathtaking indeed!

A) Questions.

1. What is an abacus?
2. How is the abacus connected with the computer?
3. Who was Charles Babbage?
4. Can you explain how Babbage's machine worked?
5. Why did his machine fail?
6. What new invention led to a breakthrough in computers?
7. Describe the Mark I.
8. Compare the Mark I with the kind of computers available today.
9. What do you think are the advantages of having computers in today's world?
10. Find out the meaning of these words: represent, essential, unwieldy, incessantly, aspect.
11. Write each of the above words in a sentence of your own.
12. Read about 'computers' in an encyclopaedia. Do a short project on the topic.

© Folens (not copiable)

Contractions

I couldn't go → I could not go

You'll see → You will see

It's six o'clock → It is six o the clock

When speaking and writing, we often shorten words by running them together.
An apostrophe (') is placed where a letter or letters have been left out.
Example: If he can't go, you'll telephone me at nine o'clock.

A) Correct the following sentences, placing an apostrophe (') where the letter or letters have been omitted.
1. Dont ask her for the new record.
2. They havent yet finished their dinner.
3. If it isnt raining, well go to the park.
4. Theyll be late coming, so lets go.
5. Id like to go to the circus but I cant.
6. Theres a boat I havent seen before in the harbour.
7. Whatever happens, dont be late for school.
8. He doesnt know wholl be playing in the football final.
9. Im going to the Halloween party.
10. Shes got the prettiest dress Ive ever seen.

B) Rewrite the following sentences, using the shortened form of the words in italics.
1. I *shall not* be able to finish my lessons this evening.
2. *Whom will* we select as captain of the school team?
3. It *does not* matter if it is raining in the afternoon.
4. *I am* sure *she will* come with us on the cycling expedition.
5. *She is* the tallest girl in my class.
6. *That is* the boy *who is* playing in the tennis final.
7. *We are* going to visit the new museum as *it is* not far from here.
8. He *did not* know the correct answer.
9. Whenever *there is* a competition, she wins.
10. *It is* cold outside and *it is* raining.

A list of common contractions.

He's ☞ he is	You've ☞ you have	Wasn't ☞ was not	Don't ☞ do not
He'd ☞ he would	You're ☞ you are	Isn't ☞ is not	We're ☞ we are
He'll ☞ he will	We've ☞ we have	Can't ☞ cannot	She's ☞ she is
I've ☞ I have	What's ☞ what is	Aren't ☞ are not	It's ☞ it is

© Folens (not copiable)

The comma

The comma indicates a brief pause.

Rules
1. It is used to indicate the person spoken to.
   Example: Hello, Vera, may I speak to your brother?
2. It is used to show a sequence of actions.
   Example: I opened the can, emptied the contents and strained the juice.
3. It is used when one writes a list of nouns or adjectives, verbs or adverbs in a sentence without employing any conjunction.
   Example: I ate a large, red, rosy apple.
4. It is used to separate phrases beginning with a present participle (......ing).
   Example: Jumping over the wall, he injured his back.
5. It is used before nouns in apposition (nouns closely related to each other).
   Example: Paris, the capital of France, is a beautiful city.

A) Use the above five rules to insert commas in each of following five sets of sentences.
1. (a) "Mary ask John for the new book."
   (b) "Ladies and Gentlemen the show is about to commence."
2. (a) Margaret yawned closed her eyes and fell asleep.
   (b) Peter stood up opened the book and began to read.
3. (a) The house was cold damp and empty.
   (b) The kangaroo jumped leaped hopped and skipped.
4. (a) Having bought a new rod I decided to go fishing.
   (b) Being the fastest runner she won the race.
5. (a) Mount Everest the highest mountain in the world was conquered by Sir Edmund Hilary and Sherpa Tensing.
   (b) Napoleon a famous general was exiled to the Island of Elba.

B) Insert the necessary commas in the following sentences.
1. I saw tigers lions monkeys and elephants at the circus.
2. We bought milk butter tea and sugar.
3. Rome Paris Madrid and London are capital cities.
4. They sold classical modern and folk records.
5. My bedroom is warm cosy and comfortable.
6. "Cheerio David until we meet again."
7. The robber snatched the money dashed out the door and escaped.
8. He washed the clothes hung them out to dry and later ironed them.
9. Feeling happy with the result I departed for London.
10. Having dug the garden she planted the seeds.

Abbreviated words

Abbreviated words: The apostrophe is placed where the letter or letters have been ommitted.
Examples: 'It'll rain tonight' means 'it will rain tonight'.
'Don't smoke' means 'do not smoke'.

A) Write out the following sentences, using the apostrophe for the words in italics.
1. *He is* a good swimmer.
2. *It is* a lovely day.
3. *I am* very lucky to have such friends.
4. *I cannot* go fishing today.
5. *We have* enjoyed our holiday.
6. *You are* welcome to come with us.
7. *I will* go to the shop for the groceries.
8. The eel *does not* like being touched.

B) The following words are common English abbreviations. Write them out in full.
1. Exam _____
2. Car _____
3. Ref _____
4. Photo _____
5. Telly _____
6. Flu _____
7. Sub _____
8. Gym _____
9. Specs _____

C) Underline the correct verb in brackets and write it in an interesting sentence.
1. The wasp (*stung, licked, pinched*) Mary on the neck.
2. The goat (*pulled, butted, spiked*) Elizabeth with his horns.
3. The hedgehog (*tickled, nibbled, prodded*) the dog with his spikes.
4. The Alsatian (*chewed, bit, munched*) my sister on the hand.
5. The hen (*pecked, gnawed, sniffed*) the little worm.
6. The jellyfish (*gulped, snorted, stung*) the girl on the leg.
7. The crab (*chewed, pinched, sucked*) me with his nippers.
8. The lion (*poisoned, devoured, smothered*) the dead zebra.
9. The bull (*caressed, gored, patted*) me with his horns.
10. The little worm (*walked, waddled, wriggled*) under the stone.
11. The pretty butterfly (*hovered, hopped, hobbled*) around the roses.
12. The eagle (*grabbed, tapped, tore*) the lamb in his talons.
13. The striped caterpillar (*staggered, crawled, toddled*) across the cabbage leaf.
14. The bullfrog (*limped, plodded, leaped*) into the marshy pond.
15. The horrid beetle (*climbed, charged, crawled*) under the mossy stone.
16. The house spider (*strolled, strode, scurried*) into his cobweb.
17. An army of crickets (*sauntered, hopped, shuffled*) about the meadow.
18. The timid snail (*flew, glided, scampered*) along the damp grass.
19. The angry wasp (*limped, flew, bounded*) over my head.
20. The busy bee (*prowled, flitted, strolled*) across the room.

© Folens (not copiable)

The cattle stampede

A) Imagine you are a cowboy in Texas. Describe an exciting cattle drive to the railroad depot.

Helpful words and phrases

the size of the herd ...... crossed rivers ...... wide plains ...... open prairies ...... weary trek ...... dangerous and difficult ...... cattle wandering ...... the hazards ...... rattlesnakes ...... buzzards ...... vultures ...... prairie wolves ...... blazing campfire ...... sing-song ...... the food ...... darkness ...... sense of danger and uneasiness ...... horse's whinny ...... flash of lightening ...... stampede ...... steers thundered past ...... the thunder of the hooves ...... clouds of dust ...... the commotion ...... the danger ...... rounding up the herd ...... counting the cost ...... eventually reaching the railroad depot ...... wages ...... celebrations ......

© Folens (not copiable)

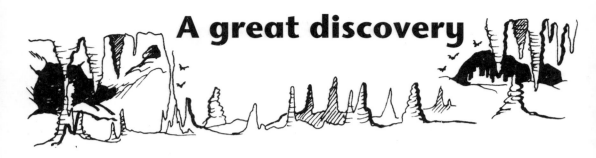

A great discovery

Jim White stopped his horse in amazement. There, straight ahead of him over the hills of New Mexico, was the most fantastic sight he had ever seen! His eagle eyes told him that the dark buzzing cloud rising from the earth was nothing other than a great mass of whirling bats. Where could they be coming from? Stooping low, the astonished cowboy made his way across the rocky ground, where he suddenly came upon a huge hole. What could be down there? Returning the next day, he began to climb down deep into the hole. Soon he saw tunnels on either side of him; so, he chose one, lit his lantern and entered. The total silence inside was eerie. When Jim shouted, the echo that returned was so powerful it almost knocked him off his feet! A few steps further and all was explained: Jim White found himself standing in a cave wide enough to hold ten football pitches and as high as a skyscraper. Hanging from the ceiling were huge icicles of stone. Great pillars, the size of trees, rose from the floor. Jim White was held spellbound by the marvellous sculptures of stone his eyes fell upon. This lucky man had discovered the Carlsbad Cavern, the largest, most spectacular and beautiful cave in the world.

On returning to the Triple X ranch that night, he wondered how such a vast cavern could have been formed. It had all begun some sixty million years earlier when water seeped through cracks on the surface and started to eat away at the solid rock underneath. The rock in this part of New Mexico was limestone, a soft rock, which is easily worn away by rainwater. Where the rock is particularly soft, huge rooms will be cut out; where the rock is fairly hard, narrow passages will be formed. Jim returned again and again to explore rooms and passageways extending for miles under the New Mexico hills. Today, tourists can retrace his footsteps through this magnificent cave, not with the aid of rope and lantern as he once did, but with lifts and electric lights. Each visitor who enters is as enthralled as Jim White was, on that day in June 1901, when he first discovered the Carlsbad Cavern.

A) Questions: Answer in sentences where possible.
1. Where did Jim White live?
2. What did he see rising from the ground one day?
3. Where did the bats come from?
4. Describe the cave he found.
5. How long does it take for such a cave to form?
6. Why did this cave form in this particular part of New Mexico?
7. How has tourism changed the cave?
8. Locate the position of New Mexico, U.S.A., on the atlas.
9. Write a list of eight words to describe how Jim White felt on first entering the Carlsbad Cavern.
10. Find out the meaning of: whirling, eerie, spectacular, seeped, extend, enthralled.
11. Write each of the above words in a sentence of your own.

© Folens (not copiable)

Word building

A) Write ten words that include the letters in the words given.

ANT	ART	OIL	ORE	ALL	OUR
1. elephant	heart	toilet	tore	small	odour
2.					
3.					
4.					
5.					
6.					
7.					
8.					
9.					
10.					

B) Change the letters of the word in capital letters to give a word with the same meaning as the phrase in the middle. The first word is completed for you.

1. OCEAN   An Indian boat.   canoe
2. MASTER   A tributary of a river.   _____
3. LEAF   A tiny insect.   _____
4. RAMP   A child's carriage.   _____
5. LAST   It flavours food.   _____
6. LUMP   A black fruit.   _____
7. ONCE   A shape like a pyramid with a round base.   _____
8. RATS   Seen in the sky at night.   _____
9. CARE   An event for athletes.   _____
10. BEARD   Food made from wheat.   _____

C) Write a suitable prefix before each word.
Examples: mistake, transport, forecast, inhuman, exchange.

1. _____ cover   9. _____ move
2. _____ form   10. _____ agree
3. _____ appear   11. _____ see
4. _____judge   12. _____ port
5. _____ rail   13. _____justice
6. _____ tell   14. _____ claim
7. _____ deed   15. _____ plant
8. _____ part

© Folens (not copiable)

More homonyms

A) Write the correct word in the appropriate space.

awl, all	1. _____ the poor shoemaker had was an _____ .
bare, bear	2. The _____ caught the man by the _____ leg.
beach, beech	3. There was a row of _____ trees near the sandy _____ .
ate, eight	4. I _____ my breakfast this morning at _____ o'clock.
two, too	5. She gave _____ apples to me _____ .
made, maid	6. The _____ told the woman that she had _____ the beds.
meet, meat	7. It is hard to _____ a butcher who sells cheap _____ .
sow, sew	8. The farmer's wife had to _____ the clothes while the farmer had to _____ the seed in the field.
one, won	9. _____ of my friends _____ first prize in the competition.
veil, vale	10. A _____ of mist hung over the _____ .
steal, steel	11. The robber tried to _____ the bars of heavy _____ .
our, hour	12. _____ bus was due to leave within the _____ .
wait, weigh	13. I had to _____ about an hour to find out the exact _____ of the jar of sweets.
week, weak	14. The girl was so _____ that she had to spend a _____ in bed.

B) 'Like' and 'unlike'

1. *steel, steal*   Which is a metal?   _____
2. *due, dew*   Which is moist?   _____
3. *pair, pare, pear*   Which is a fruit?   _____
4. *sell, cell*   Which is a prison room?   _____
5. *course, coarse*   Which is rough?   _____
6. *grate, great*   Which one has to do with fire?   _____
7. *foul, fowl*   Which is the bird?   _____
8. *cannon, canon*   Which is a gun?   _____

Exercises

A) Write the opposite of the verbs in italics.

1. The man *opened* the stable door.   _____
2. The farmer *sold* the pig.   _____
3. The hen *sat on* the eggs.   _____
4. The shepherd *hated* his work.   _____
5. The tractor *arrived* on time.   _____
6. The horse *raised* his head.   _____

© Folens (not copiable)

Prepositions

A 'preposition' is a word which shows the relation between two other words.
For example: The key is *over* the door. The mouse is *under* the box.

A) Fill in the blank spaces with a suitable preposition from the given list.
(beside, over, off, on, towards, at, into, down, of, in, by, to, through, against, with, under, up, from, for, between)

1. The helicopter flew _____ the mountains and landed _____ the beach.
2. Last year I climbed _____ Mount Brandon _____ my best friend.
3. He went _____ the hardware shop and bought a tin _____ paint.
4. The library closed _____ an hour _____ one and two o'clock.
5. Neil jumped _____ the wall and ran _____ the gate.
6. We sheltered _____ a tree _____ the rain.
7. They sailed _____ the South Pacific _____ a large yacht.
8. Arsenal played _____ Everton last Sunday and lost _____ a goal.
9. They escaped _____ the exit door and ran _____ the fire-escape.
10. I will meet you _____ the shop _____ the railway station.

B) Many prepositions are used after verbs. Write the various prepositions which could be used after each of the following verbs.

1. walk
2. listen
3. argue
4. came
5. look
6. pick
7. stand
8. smash
9. talk

Compound words

A compound word is made up of two or more separate words.
For example: ash+tray= ashtray

A) Complete the following words in order to form compound words.

1. _____ board
2. _____ man
3. _____ post
4. _____ case
5. _____ cup
6. _____ keeper
7. _____ father
8. _____ port
9. _____ ball
10. _____ mine
11. _____ cloth
12. _____ wreck

Useful words and expressions

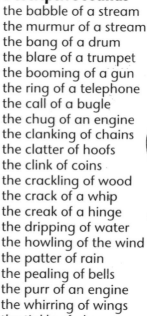

1. Anger
to be angry
to be annoyed
to be furious
to be cross
to be vexed
to be provoked
to be in a rage
to be in a violent temper

13/5

2. Fatigue
to be tired
to be exhausted
to be worn out
to be weary
to be puffed out
to be as weak as water

3. Fear
to be afraid
to be scared
to be terrified
to be frightened
to be alarmed
to be shaking with fear
to be shivering with terror
to be apprehensive

4. Sadness
to be sad
to be miserable
to be lonesome
to be unhappy
to be distressed
to be depressed
to be gloomy
to be dejected
to be mournful
to be broken-hearted
to feel wretched

5. Joy and happiness
to be happy
to be joyful
to be contented
to be cheerful
to be jolly
to be good-humoured
to be delighted

6. Descriptive sounds
the babble of a stream
the murmur of a stream
the bang of a drum
the blare of a trumpet
the booming of a gun
the ring of a telephone
the call of a bugle
the chug of an engine
the clanking of chains
the clatter of hoofs
the clink of coins
the crackling of wood
the crack of a whip
the creak of a hinge
the dripping of water
the howling of the wind
the patter of rain
the pealing of bells
the purr of an engine
the whirring of wings
the tinkle of glass
the swish of skirts
the rustling of silk (leaves)
the wail of the siren
the popping of corks
the rumble of a train
the tick of a clock
the sighing of the wind
the roar of the torrent
the slam of a door
the tramp of feet
the shuffling of feet

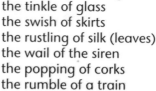

94

© Folens (not copiable)

7. Quickness of movement

suddenly
at once
quickly
instantly
immediately
hurriedly
promptly
in a flash
in the twinkling of an eye

8. Group terms

a cluster of stars
a bouquet of flowers
a clutch of eggs
a bunch of grapes
a forest of trees
a suit of clothes
a suite of furniture
a fleet of ships
a clump of trees
an army of soldiers
a company of actors
a team of players
a troupe of dancers
a host of angels
a crew of sailors
a choir of singers
a band of musicians
a party of friends

9. Weather

a fine day
a sunny day
a bright day
a splendid day
a gorgeous day
a glorious day
a beautiful day
a pleasant day
a warm day
a windy day
a rainy day
It's windy
It's raining heavily
It's pouring rain
It's snowing heavily
It's horrible weather
It's freezing hard
It's stormy
It's dreadful weather
It's cloudy

10. Crowds

a huge crowd
a great multitude
a mass of people
thronged with ...
crowded with ...
black with ...
swarming with ...
teeming with ...
dotted with ...
a street mob
a church congregation
football spectators
a concert audience

11. Diminutive phrases

a grain of sugar
a grain of sand
a pinch of tea
a pinch of snuff
a pinch of pepper
a sip of water
a pat of butter
a crumb of bread
a morsel of food
a ray of sunshine
a beam of light
a puff of wind
a breath of air
a flake of snow
a drop of rain
a wisp of smoke
a blade of grass
a posy of flowers
a strand of hair
a speck of dust
a dab of paint
a tint of colour
a chip of wood
a splinter of glass
a gust of wind
a particle of dust

12. Comparisons

as old as the hills
as fast as a hare
as black as coal
as heavy as lead
as meek as a lamb
as fresh as a daisy
as strong as an ox
as swift as a deer
as hungry as a wolf
as graceful as a swan
as poor as a church mouse
as weak as water
as pale as death
as quick as lightning
as clean as a new pin
as clear as crystal
as silent as the grave
as white as a sheet
as busy as an ant
as brown as a berry
as soft as putty

13. Exclamations

Oh!
Alas!
Ouch!
What !
Look out!
Oh dear!
Hush!
Nonsense!
Fire!
Bravo!

Hurrah!
Hello!
Help!
Hark!
Ahoy!
Good gracious!

14. Commonly misspelt words

already
altogether
amount
Arctic
beggar
believe
beautiful
bicycle
careful
chief
century
died
disappear
except
experience
family
forty
friend
guard
hero
humour
interested
jealous
meant
minute
prove

15. Common contractions

The apostrophe is placed where the letter or letters have been omitted. *He's* means *He is*

He's	He is	What's	What is
He'd	He would	Wasn't	Was not
He'll	He will	Isn't	Is it not
I've	I have	Hadn't	Had not
I'll	I will	Can't	Cannot
You've	You have	Aren't	Are not
You'll	You will	Didn't	Did not
You'd	You would	Won't	Will not
You're	You are	Don't	Do not
We've	We have	Doesn't	Does not
They'll	They will	Shan't	Shall not

WORD POWER

© Folens (not copiable)